LATIN
LOVE
LESSONS

LATIN
LOVE
LESSONS

Put a Little Ovid in Your Life

Charlotte Higgins

HARPER

An Imprint of HarperCollins *Publishers*

www.harpercollins.com

HarperCollins books may be purchased for educational, business, or sales promotional use. For information please write: Special Markets Department, HarperCollins Publishers, 10 East 53rd Street, New York, NY 10022.

Originally published in Great Britain in 2007 by Short Books.

FIRST U.S. EDITION

Library of Congress Cataloging-in-Publication Data is available upon request.

ISBN 978-0-06-154742-3

09 10 11 12 13 OFF/RRD 10 9 8 7 6 5 4 3 2 1

uulpi carissimae

INTRODUCTION

What can a bunch of 2,000-year-old poems in Latin teach us about love in the twenty-first century?

Actually, pretty much everything. The Romans didn't only build great cities, dominate the known world, and bring us straight roads. They were also the original, and best, Latin lovers.

Take this tiny, two-line poem, by Catullus.

> *Odi et amo. Quare id faciam, fortasse requiris?*
> *nescio, sed fieri sentio, et excrucior*

> I hate and love. Why do I do this, perhaps you ask?
> I don't know. But I feel it's being done to me, and
> the pain is crucifixion.

In fourteen words Catullus nails the feelings you have when you're in love with the wrong person. You hate them, you love them; you know you could, and should, wrench yourself away, but you can't. The pain is killing you.

When I first read poems like this as a teenager I marvelled at their frankness and immediacy. Now, two decades on, and having experienced rather more of life and break-ups than I had at fifteen, I'm gripped more than ever: it seems miraculous that a stranger writing two millennia back could pin down an emotional state with such uncanny accuracy; but he did. It's like what Hector – the marvellous old-buffer teacher in Alan Bennett's play *The History Boys* – says:

> "The best moments in reading are when you come across something – a thought, a feeling, a way of looking at things – which you had thought special and particular to you. Now here it is, set down by someone else ... someone even who is long dead. And it is as if a hand has come out and taken yours."

To realise that strong and painful feelings are not particular, but shared – that is the beginning of recovery. Unlikely as it may seem, Latin poetry can help mend a broken heart, I discovered.

Catullus is the tip of the iceberg. With Ovid (whose voice is so immediate, urbane and witty you feel you could bump into him at a party tonight) you can discover how to find a lover, cure yourself of love, and even pick up a few sex tips. With Virgil, you can be given an object lesson in how not to treat a girlfriend or boyfriend. With Propertius, experience the traumas of obsession, and encounter an almost Proustian determination to express precisely what being in love feels like. With Horace, learn how to grasp life by the balls and live it to the full.

By the way, you don't need to know Latin to appreciate these works. Throughout this book, I've provided poems in the original language as well as in translation. If you know even a tiny bit of Latin, or even a smattering of French or Spanish, you'll be able to piece together something of how the Latin works. Equally, the English translations on their own are an excellent way into this world of extraordinary writing – some of the most powerful poetry ever produced.

The Rome these people lived in is always there in the background of these poems, too: hugely wealthy, massively materialist, giddyingly cosmopolitan, and full of disposable but addictive pleasures – not so far removed from the New York or London of our own times, in some ways. In fact we are probably better placed than readers from any other period in modern history to understand the preoccupations of these writers. Like the Romans of Horace and Ovid's time, we live a life of conspicuous consumption while much of the rest of the world struggles for survival. The Romans wrote a great deal about their craving for *"luxuria"*, "luxury"; they simultaneously indulged their gluttonous appetite for fabulous houses, expensive clothes and exotic foods while harking back nostalgically to the good old days when life had been simpler and we weren't all on our way to hell in a handcart. The Romans' heightened sense of the individual, and of personal ambition, seems uncannily familiar in these self-fulfilment-obsessed times. And we're certainly one of the first generations to be able to connect comfortably with their frankness about sex (straight and gay), which has historically been a huge problem for readers coming from a Judaeo-Christian perspective, particularly in the nineteenth and early twentieth centuries.

Twenty-first-century New York and Rome in the first century BC – not as different as you might think . . .

The Romans, then, have a great deal to teach us about love. Certainly more than the reams of depressing self-help books that populate the shelves of bookshops (the Latin poets, it hardly needs saying, are an infinitely classier read). Ovid's poems the *Ars Amatoria* (*The Art of Love*) and the *Remedia Amoris* (*The Cures For Love*) are blatantly "how-to" books – how to find and keep a lover; and how to get over love. There are plenty of books on this kind of thing in the Mind, Body, Spirit aisle, but, frankly, you won't get any funnier, wiser or more sophisticated than Ovid. Even Propertius, from the depths of his obsession, reckons his books are useful for modern lovers. "*Me legat assidue post haec neglectus amator,/et prosint illi cognita nostra mala*," he writes – "Let neglected lovers read me assiduously in the future; and find help, understanding my troubles."

Most books written about these poems are academic, and occasionally unbelievably dry, works of literary criticism. No serious scholar would stoop to writing about them as if they were about actual emotions. And yet it seems abundantly clear to me, as I am sure it does to anyone else who reads them, that they are – vividly so. That is really what this book is about.

Now for a little background history. All the poems in this book come from the period spanning the end of the Roman Republic and the beginning of the Empire. It was a golden age for literature, and the most incredible, and turbulent, age in history. It didn't all turn on politics and war, either. Rome, as her empire grew bigger, and bigger, underwent huge social – and sexual – changes.

The citizens of the Roman Republic had traditionally been proud of their prudery. As far as moralists were concerned, the ideal Roman was tough, self-denying and ascetic. As for women – well, divorcing your wife simply because she ventured out of doors without her head veiled was perfectly acceptable; in theory, she was expected to be at home, weaving wool for the family and raising model citizens: good soldiers, good politicians, good farmers.

But in the first century BC all those certainties – though they continued to be endlessly articulated by Roman writers and moralists – were thrown to the winds. By the lifetime of giants of history such as Julius Caesar, Mark Antony and Octavian, contact with decadent Greeks and other fun-loving eastern Mediterranean types had brought an unstoppable craze for pleasure and luxury to Rome. I say contact with: I ought to say crushing of. The startling military success of the swiftly growing Empire was coupled with a ruthless stripping of defeated nations' assets. Money flooded into Rome. After the great general Sulla put down a rebellion in Athens in 86 BC, to take but one example, he calmly shipped her movables back home: complete libraries, endless amounts of priceless sculpture, even living athletes were brought to Italy.

This wholesale pillaging, this forced transport of goods and ideas from the most cultured nation on earth, helped create the circumstances under which Roman poets really began to flourish. For the Greeks had more than high art going for them: their culture of elaborate dinner parties, or *symposia*, with delicious food and wine, music, and the company of gorgeous girls and boys, was already all the rage in Rome. Sulla himself, a highly successful, driven and at times chillingly cruel military leader, was said to enjoy wild parties and the company of singers, actors and tarts.

As this bullish little city brought to heel more and more foreign nations, it began to be shaken by political turbulence on a devastating scale at home. In 81 BC, Sulla became sole dictator, brutally overturning four centuries of proudly polished republican ideology. Even though he resigned his dictatorship in 79 BC, the door to absolute rule had been opened a chink.

Over subsequent decades, Rome was swallowed by civil war again, victim of the power struggles of highly ambitious and ruthless men. In the 50s, the city was torn apart by civil disorder, and in 49 BC, Julius Caesar crossed the Rubicon and waged a civil war with Pompey the Great. Caesar triumphed and became dictator – before being assassinated on the Ides of March, 44 BC. Rome's stability would be restored only when the young Octavian, great-nephew of Caesar, managed to step clear of the car crash of Rome's strife, having crushed his great-uncle's assassins, and finally his former ally, Mark Antony, at the Battle of Actium in 31 BC. In all this, hundreds of thousands of citizens were killed. Estates were confiscated, murder on a huge scale was sanctioned by whoever happened to have the upper hand at the time. Between 42 and 41 BC alone, it is estimated that 150 senators and 2,000 members of the equestrian class were killed.

Octavian's victory at the Battle of Actium brought an end to the strife, at long last. He declared the "*res publica restituta*", "the Republic restored", in 27 BC. But it was a shallow claim. He became "*imperator Augustus*", "the emperor Augustus", and was accorded unprecedented personal powers. The city had exchanged one political system for another. Four centuries after triumphantly expelling their kings, worn out by civil war, the citizens had ended up once more with a sole ruler.

This age of political revolution was also an age of extraordinary, larger-than-life love affairs – of which Mark Antony's famous liaison with Cleopatra was only the most scandalous. The new culture of pleasure and sophistication brought with it the idea of falling in love as a lifestyle choice. Aristocratic ladies started behaving not like the veiled, stern matrons supposed to exemplify Roman womanhood, but like glamorous Greek courtesans. Take Clodia Metelli, for instance. She was from one of the very grandest Roman families, the Claudians. She and her sisters and brothers affected a plebeian-style spelling of their family name, slumming it as an outrageous fashion statement. Clodia was married to one of the greatest politicians in the land, whom, rumour had it, she poisoned. She was as famous for her affairs as for her beauty, throwing scandalous parties, picking up boys, and taking trips to Baiae, a seaside resort near Naples with a reputation for forbidden pleasures on tap.

Annoyingly perhaps for Mark Antony,
Julius Caesar got in there first ...

Julius Caesar was also famous for his love affairs, and years before Mark Antony got in there, he made it with the clever, charming, polyglot Cleopatra. Indeed, Caesar once blew a whole fortune to buy a single, vast pearl for his favourite mistress, Servilia (played by Lindsay Duncan in the terrific TV series *Rome*).

The Roman love poets I'm writing about all emerged from

this period of enormous turbulance and political change. Catullus was the earliest, born in 84 BC – three years before Sulla declared himself dictator – in Verona, son of a well-off provincial family. As a young man, he settled in Rome, and became one of the party-set. Many scholars believe the Lesbia he addressed in his love poems was really Clodia Metelli, veiled by a pseudonym. From Catullus's poems, we get glimpses of his life and tastes: that he has a taste for the sort of elegant, learned, Greek-language poetry written in Alexandria two centuries before; that he is friends with the highly fashionable aesthetes who shared his artistic preoccupations. He goes to parties, falls for boys, scrapes around for money, gets bitchy (and writes the rudest, funniest, most obscene poems about his enemies). He doesn't give a toss about Julius Caesar. He likes the spring; he's fond of his brother. He has a certain nostalgia for his roots, up north in Verona. The hundred-odd poems he left us seem all the more miraculous for the fact that he was probably only about 30 when he died. No one had ever before written love poems like the 25 or so he wrote about Lesbia. The Greeks, it's true, wrote wonderfully about desire, but Catullus was the first person in history to write in a sustained way about the whole trajectory of a love affair, through its opening salvos to its agonising descent into bitterness.

Nearly all the other poets I quote in this book were a generation younger than Catullus. Propertius was born in around 54 BC, so was a toddler when the older poet died. His family was equestrian – the rank immediately beneath senatorial, which was as grand as you got in Rome – but had suffered in some of the land confiscations of the civil wars. His first book of elegies, which concentrates on his beautiful, wilful, stubborn mistress Cynthia, came out in the early 20s, around a decade after Augustus had emerged as the sole leader of Rome. Its very first word, in fact, is Cynthia – signalling his total obsession. In his poems he traced and retraced the shape of his relationship in an attempt to capture the fugitive essence of desire.

After the book was published, Propertius was drawn into the milieu of the Etruscan millionaire Maecenas, confidant of Augustus, and Rome's most important literary patron. Maecenas was a silk-clad, jewellery-laden hedonist; a gourmet who was said to have introduced the exotic dish of young donkey flesh to a doubtless grateful Rome. More importantly, he formed a welcome buffer zone between the poets and Augustus. The emperor, we can infer, wanted grand, epic poems that would glorify his reign, the sort of thing that Greek dynasts had in past centuries ordered by the yard. It seems that the poets were, on the whole, less than keen to comply. Maecenas tactfully negotiated the independence of the poets against the demands of the emperor, until his influence began to fade from around the early 20s BC.

Virgil was also part of the circle of Maecenas. A north Italian provincial like Catullus, he was born in Mantua in 70 BC, to a well-off but not super-grand family. He lived till he was 51; and for nineteen of those years Rome was tearing itself apart in civil war. In the period right after Julius Caesar's assassination he wrote a series of exquisite pastoral poems, the *Eclogues*. About a decade later, when Augustus was beginning to establish himself after Actium, came the 2,000-line poem the *Georgics*. Ostensibly a didactic poem about farming, it is tinged with reflection about the ethics of rural life and with affection for the Italian countryside. When Virgil died in 19 BC the *Aeneid* was not quite finished after ten years of work. If this was supposed to fulfil Augustus's desire for an epic in praise of his achievements, it did so only obliquely, since, though it casts forward to the Augustan present at times, its hero is the mythical founder of the Roman people, the Trojan hero Aeneas. In this poem he gives us the love story of Dido and Aeneas, one of the great doomed romances of all time, in which love is pitted against duty – and loses.

Tibullus was born about two years after Propertius, and, like Propertius, he was an equestrian, and again one who complained of straitened circumstances. According to an anonymous biography, he was handsome and an extremely snappy dresser. His first book of poetry came out shortly after Propertius's. He was not part of Maecenas's circle; his patron was another grandee, the statesman, orator and soldier Marcus Valerius Messalla Corvinus – whose niece, Sulpicia, was responsible for the only surviving poems (and just six at that) written by a woman in Rome, which have been passed down to us along with Tibullus's work.

Of all the Latin love poets, Horace was from the humblest background. A little older than Propertius and Tibullus, he was born in what is now Puglia, in southern Italy, in 65 BC. His father was a freedman tax collector, though well-enough off to send his son to be expensively educated in Rome. Horace fought on the "wrong side" at the Battle of Philippi, the conflict at which Octavian and Mark Antony defeated Brutus and Cassius in 42 BC – but he redeemed himself sufficiently that in about 38 BC he began to be drawn under Maecenas's wing. His work is effortlessly wide-ranging, spanning politics, ethics, literary criticism, philosophy – and love. Unlike poets such as Propertius and Catullus, though, he didn't write about the traumas and triumphs of relationships, composing poem after poem about the same women. You get a sense of casual, if often affectionate, encounters; that love is a light-hearted affair to be treated with a certain irony. His first book of odes came out in 24–23 BC; he wrote four books of odes in total, as well as satires and epistles. He died in 8 BC, the same year as his patron and great friend Maecenas.

Finally comes Ovid. He was the last to be born of our poets, in Sulmona in central Italy in 43 BC, the year after Caesar was assassinated. He was twelve when Octavian won the battle of Actium, so the traumas of civil war, though recent, were not quite the vivid realities to him that they were to his older colleagues. Another well-off equestrian, his early training was in the law, but he quickly gave that up to devote himself full-time to poetry. The *Amores,* his love elegies, were his earliest works. His *Ars Amatoria*, or *Art of Love*, which I draw on heavily in this book, was published around the time of Christ's birth; and his magnum opus, the wonderful, baroque poem *Metamorphoses*, about mythical transformations, was substantially finished around AD 8. But that same year he was disgraced under mysterious circumstances, and banished by Augustus to the Black Sea. There, a decade later, he died – and with him the last of an astonishing stream of love poetry that has, arguably, never yet been bettered.

From the best chat-up lines to the most percipient advice on how to get over a break-up; from grooming tips to sex tips; not to mention the most emotionally rich writing on the feelings that being in love gives us: it's all here in the poems of these writers. So read on: it's time to become a Latin lover!

I. CARPE DIEM

Uiuamus, mea Lesbia, atque amemus
Let us live and love, my Lesbia
Catullus, Poem Five

In Saul Bellow's masterpiece *Seize the Day*, the three-parts charlatan, one-part visionary Dr. Tamkin, a *soi-disant* psychologist, explains the following to the hapless hero, Wilhelm:

> "The spiritual compensation is what I look for. Bringing people into the here-and-now. The real universe. That's the present moment. The past is no good to us. The future is full of anxiety. Only the present is real—the here-and-now. Seize the day."

Later, he offers the following rather hilarious advice:

> "You should try some of my 'here-and-now' mental exercises. It stops you from thinking so much about the future and the past and cuts down confusion."

As much as I love the idea of "here-and-now" exercises, this wasn't what Horace had in mind at all when he wrote his great Ode 1.11, in which he set down the immortal phrase "carpe diem", seize the day. In fact the thrust of his poem, if one can be forgiven for boiling down a great poem into a single crude sentiment, is: "Let's go to bed, right now." Don't let your chance slip by, says the poet. Who knows how long we've got left?

Let's have the Latin:

Tu ne quaesieris – scire nefas – quem mihi, quem tibi
finem di dederint, Leuconoë, nec Babylonios
temptaris numeros. ut melius, quicquid erit, pati!
seu plures hiemes, seu tribuit Iuppiter ultimam,
quae nunc oppositis debilitat pumicibus mare
Tyrrhenum. sapias, vina liques, et spatio breui
spem longam reseces. dum loquimur, fugerit inuida
aetas: carpe diem, quam minimum credula postero.

Don't ask what end the gods have laid down for us, Leuconoë, it's wrong to ask: don't play with Babylonian horoscopes. It's much better to put up with whatever comes, whether Jupiter grants us more winters, or whether this is the last now exhausting the Mediterranean on the cliffs that block its waves. Be wise, strain the wine, and prune back your hopes to the short term. While we're talking, jealous time has already fled: seize the day and put as little trust as possible in tomorrow.

We don't know anything about Leuconoë, to whom this poem is addressed: whether her name means she was Greek, or whether it's a pseudonym for someone Roman; whether she is a slave or a freedwoman or a courtesan or not; whether she even existed. Not that it really matters. The set-up is this: she is anxiously checking their horoscopes to try to figure out how long she and Horace each have left on this mortal coil. But there's no point, says Horace – we can't know what's in store for us, and we shouldn't try to find out. We may be carried off tomorrow, for all we know. In fact, we're wasting time even having this conversation. Let's go to bed. And while you're at it, pour us a drink – "*uina liques*", or, literally, "strain the wine". (I have one translation that gives this phrase as "busy thyself with household tasks", which always gives me the giggles, since it seems to suggest that Leuconoë pause for a spot of dusting, not my idea of "*carpe diem*" at all.)

The point is, if you use "*carpe diem*" to try to get someone into bed – as innumerable lovers have undoubtedly done since 23 BC when this poem was published – you are behaving entirely within the spirit of Horace, who, despite being projected by many Latin teachers as a sort of suburban worthy, impeccable as to his personal virtues, was a bit of a shagger, even to the extent of being given the rather compromising nickname "*purissimus penis*", or "purest penis", by the emperor Augustus.

The word "*carpe*" – "gather", "harvest" – is often used of plucking flowers; and plucking flowers in ancient literature is, well, nearly always an erotic metaphor. People pluck each other's virginity in ancient literature like there was no tomorrow. So congratulations, keep it up, and I am sure it is extremely effective. Those of you who have not used "*carpe diem*", do consider adding it to your armoury, in translation if your audience requires it. (And remember, have safe sex at all times, if you really are planning on enjoying "*plures hiemes*", "more winters".)

As it happens, the first ever episode of *Buffy the Vampire Slayer* has its "*carpe diem*" moment, courtesy of writer Joss Whedon; and it is pretty close to the original spirit of the phrase.

In the Bronze, Sunnydale's one and only nightclub, Buffy is chatting to her new schoolfriend, Willow, who is explaining that she finds dating hard, since she happens to be struck by a paralysing shyness in the presence of boys whom she finds attractive. Buffy offers the following advice:

Buffy: Well, my philosophy . . . Do you want to hear my philosophy?
Willow: Yeah, I do.
Buffy: Life is short.
Willow: Life is short?

Buffy: Not original, I grant you, but it's true. Why waste time being all shy and wondering if some guy is going to laugh at you? Seize the moment – because tomorrow you might be dead.

The joke here is that they both happen to have a very strong chance indeed of being dead tomorrow since, unbeknown to Willow, they are living atop the mouth of Hell in a town awash with vampires and demons. There's another twist, too: a few moments later, we see Buffy talking to her Watcher (a sort of mentor and adviser), who accuses her of insufficient commitment to her calling as the Vampire Slayer. Can she, for instance, sense if there are any vampires here now? Yes, says Buffy, there's one over there, I can tell by his outfit ("It's dated?" suggests Giles, the Watcher. "It's carbon-dated. Trust me, only someone living underground for ten years would think that was still a look," confirms Buffy). But suddenly, Buffy realises that the girl the vampire is chatting up is Willow – who's busily acting on Buffy's advice to seize the moment, and thus well on her way to a grisly death by vampiric kiss.

It is necessary here to point out that acting within the spirit of "*carpe diem*" is not without its pitfalls. Seize the day, yes – but don't behave like a complete idiot.

There is another instance of the phrase that I have a soft

spot for – although it's missing the point of "*carpe diem*" – in *Clueless* (1995). In this masterpiece of modern cinema, a witty take on Jane Austen's *Emma*, the fabulous but flawed Cher (Alicia Silverstone) is out shopping at the mall with the Frank Churchill character, Christian, now transmuted from love interest into gay best friend.

> Christian: This jacket. Is it Jason Priestley, or James Dean?
> Cher: *Carpe diem!* You look hot in it.

You have to imagine *carpe diem* as carp-ay diy-em, in the full glory of her Californian accent.

I suppose if we're on films, I have to mention That Speech, given by Robin Williams, as teacher John Keating, in *Dead Poets Society* (sic – they never gave those poor poets an apostrophe). It's a little too Dr. Tamkin for me, alas. If you'll recall, Professor Keating is trying to inspire the posh schoolboys in his care to follow the example of the dead poets: to ignore dull convention and the status quo.

> "They're not that different from you, are they? Same hair-cuts. Full of hormones, just like you. Invincible, just like you feel. The world is their oyster. They believe they're destined for great things, just like many of you, their eyes are full of hope, just like you. Did they wait until it was too late to

make from their lives even one iota of what they were capable? Because, you see gentlemen, these boys are now fertilising daffodils. But if you listen real close, you can hear them whisper their legacy to you. Go on, lean in. Listen, you hear it – *Carpe* – hear it? – *Carpe, carpe diem*, seize the day, boys, make your lives extraordinary."

Back to sex, mercifully – another side of the sentiment, "let's get on with it now", is "don't waste your youth" – as in the Clown's song in Shakespeare's *Twelfth Night*:

What is love? 'Tis not hereafter;
Present mirth has present laughter;
What's to come is still unsure.
In delay there lies no plenty,
Then come and kiss me sweet and twenty;
Youth's a stuff will not endure.

That Speech by Robin Williams

The lovely Young Vic Theatre in London nearly had "Youth's a stuff will not endure" inscribed around its bar area both as a delicate reminder of mortality (Young Vic/Youth's a stuff . . . get it?) and as a healthy incitement to debauchery to its punters. Then they decided it was a bit too pretentious.

The poet Tibullus had this to say in a similar spirit. This is from the first poem of his first book of elegies (published in 27 BC). Many of his love poems are addressed to a woman called Delia (though there's also another girlfriend with the cheerful name Nemesis, not a good egg by all accounts, and a boyfriend called Marathus).

> *interea, dum fata sinunt, iungamus amores:*
> *iam ueniet tenebris Mors adoperta caput;*
> *iam subrepet iners aetas, neque amare decebit,*
> *dicere nec cano blanditias capite.*

> Meanwhile, with Fate's permission, let us unite and love.
> Tomorrow Death will come, head hooded in the dark,
> or useless Age creep up, and will not be seemly
> to make white-headed love or pretty speeches.

> [Guy Lee]

Up to a point, Tibullus, though if you are contemplating a long-term, till-death-us-do-part relationship, white-headed love in "*iners aetas*", "useless old age", will be just the thing.

Even more urgently Robert Herrick, in his *"To the Virgins, to Make Much of Time"*, suggests:

Gather ye rosebuds while ye may,
Old Time is still a-flying:
And this same flower that smiles to-day
To-morrow will be dying.

He puts a sting in the tail in that last line. Time is rushing on; it's a short step from smiling to dying. It's not entirely unlike Ovid's cheeky version of the thought in the third book of his *Ars Amatoria*, where the idea of *"carpe diem"* is turned into a piece of rather cynical advice on pulling-technique for the ladies (really, one suspects here, handed out for the benefit of men). His message? Get out there, girls, and have fun, before you lose your looks: it's easier to get laid if you're young and haven't ruined your figure already with babies. After all, you're going to end up a withered old hag sleeping alone in bed at night in no time at all. (I am sure you will join me in thanking Ovid for the reminder that sagging skin, a Zimmer frame and incontinence pads are only just round the corner.)

quam cito, me miserum, laxantur corpora rugis
    et perit, in nitido qui fuit ore, color,
quasque fuisse tibi canas a uirgine iures

29

sparguntur subito per caput omne comae!
anguibus exuitur tenui cum pelle uetustas,
nec faciunt ceruos cornua iacta senes;
nostra sine auxilio fugiunt bona: carpite florem,
qui, nisi carptus erit, turpiter ipse cadet.
adde, quod et partus faciunt breuiora iuuentae
tempora: continua messe senescit ager.

Ars Amatoria III, ll. 73–82

Too soon – ah, horror! –
Flesh goes slack and wrinkled, the clear
Complexion is lost, those white streaks you swear date
                                    back to
Your schooldays suddenly spread,
You're grey-haired. A snake husks off old age with its fragile
Discarded skin; cast horns
Leave the stag in its prime. Unaided, a woman's charms will
Vanish away. Pluck the flower; left unplucked
It will wither and fall. Youth's span is shortened yet further
By childbirth: overcropping ages a field.

[Peter Green]

He takes the "*carpe diem*" thought to its rather unpleasant conclusion – that is, if you don't "*carpite florem*", "pluck the flower" – it will wither on the bough. (Unplucked, you wither on the the bough; plucked, you risk being overharvested; who said it wasn't tough being a woman?)

Much more cheerfully in the spirit of "let's get on with it" is the marvellous Catullus Poem Five, one of the most justly famous poems in ancient literature. Addressed to his girlfriend Lesbia, it's a fabulous manifesto for grasping life by the balls and getting on with love, no matter what petty disapproval one might encounter from bitter and jealous naysayers along the way. The first line alone will suffice as a seduction.

Viuamus, mea Lesbia, atque amemus
rumoresque senum seueriorum
omnes unius aestimemus assis.
soles occidere et redire possunt;
nobis, cum semel occidit breuis lux,
nox est perpetua una dormienda.
da mi basia mille, deinde centum,
dein mille altera, dein secunda centum,
deinde usque altera mille, deinde centum.
dein cum milia multa fecerimus,
conturbabimus illa, ne sciamus
aut ne quis malus inuidere possit,
cum tantum sciat esse basiorum.

My Lesbia, let us live and love
And not care tuppence for old men
Who sermonise and disapprove.
Suns when they sink can rise again,

But we, when our brief light has shone,
Must sleep the long night on and on.
Kiss me: a thousand kisses, then
A hundred more, and now a second
Thousand and hundred, and now still
Hundreds and thousands more, until
The thousand thousands can't be reckoned
And we've lost track of the amount
And nobody can work us ill
With the evil eye by keeping count.

[James Michie]

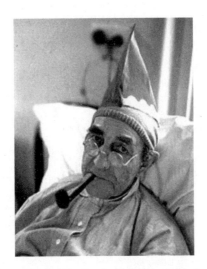

*Don't care tuppence for the disapproval of
grumpy old men, says Catullus*

This is a rather nice version of the opening lines by the sixteenth/seventeenth-century poet and composer Thomas Campion, the first stanza of a longer poem:

My sweetest Lesbia, let us live and love,
And, though the sager sort our deedes reprove,
Let us not way them: heavn's great lampes doe dive
Unto their west, and strait againe revive,
But, soone as once set is our little light,
Then must we sleepe one ever-during night.

Viuamus atque amemus: let us live and love. A motto worth sticking to.

II. OVID'S THREE-STEP PULLING PROGRAMME

arte regendus Amor
Love: it's all in the technique
Ovid, *Ars Amatoria* I

Fortunately for the aspirant Latin lover, the Romans left us a long, detailed, scandalous, hilarious, cynical, explicit and still incredibly user-friendly handbook on how to go about finding, and keeping, the man or woman of our dreams. Ovid's fabulous poem, the *Ars Amatoria,* or *The Art of Love*, was first published around the time that Jesus Christ was teething on the other side of the Mediterranean. And it's still up to its job better than the stuff you'll find in your local bookshop's self-help section.

The *Ars* is the ancient equivalent of a how-to book. It is a didactic poem, that is, a poem meant to teach you something. Its forebears in the genre of didactic poetry tended to be about utterly respectable things such as farming (the Greek poet Hesiod's *Works and Days*; Virgil's *Georgics*) and the natural sciences (Lucretius's *On the Nature of the Universe*). Ovid's *Ars Amatoria* is quite a different proposition. Instead of teaching you the right season to prune your vines, or how atoms work, it is full of brilliant information on sexual positions and how to apply make-up to maximise your pulling power. Ovid had taken a serious, learned, literary genre, and done something daringly racy and sexy with it.

Alas, the poem was off-message as far as the emperor was concerned. Augustus, despite a youth full of exuberant philandering, had become rather family-values obsessed by the time it was published, probably between 2 BC and AD 2. In *I, Claudius*, the marvellous 1976 TV epic adapted from Robert Graves's novels, Augustus, in the inimitable booming tones of the mighty Brian Blessed, is heard to utter of Ovid:

> "I've never liked that man. All right, his poetry's very beautiful. But it's also very smutty. A lot of it's downright indecent. Frankly, I wouldn't have him in the house . . . write poetry, yes, but write about nice things, things that you'd like your family to hear."

Total invention, of course, but not entirely implausible.

In AD 8 Augustus made his disapproval felt: he banished poor Ovid to the remote and deeply provincial Tomis on the Black Sea, now the resort of Constanta, in Romania (and still not necessarily a place you'd want to spend a whole decade of your life). Despite the fact that his wife stayed in Rome, lobbying for his pardon, Ovid never made it back, and died there in AD 18. According to Ovid's rather elliptical account of all this, the reason he was sent away from his beloved

Rome was "*carmen et error*", a poem and a mistake. The poem was the *Ars*, and as for the "mistake", it was presumably some kind of sexual or political peccadillo, thought by some to be connected with Augustus's banishment of his own granddaughter Julia for adultery that same year.

Brian Blessed's memorable Augustus

That's enough history; it's time to get down to the important business of how to get laid, Roman style. There are three steps in Ovid's brilliant pulling programme: preparation; how to meet potential partners; and continuing contact.

Ovid's step one: preparation

Appearance is all-important in the drive to attract a mate. As every marketing expert knows, attractive packaging is half the battle when it comes to selling a product. So it's time to consider a makeover. This goes for women and men, since the *Ars Amatoria,* helpfully, has separate sections for each – it's in three books: the first is aimed at men trying to find girls; the second is on how to hang on to your lover; and the third is for women on the look-out for men.

First, boys:

munditie placeant, fuscentur corpora Campo;
  sit bene conueniens et sine labe toga.
lingua nec rigeat; careant rubigine dentes;
  nec uagus in laxa pes tibi pelle natet.
nec male deformet rigidos tonsura capillos:
  sit coma, sit trita barba resecta manu.
et nihil emineant et sint sine sordibus ungues,
  inque caua nullus stet tibi nare pilus.
nec male odorati sit tristis anhelitus oris,
  nec laedat nares uirque paterque gregis.
cetera lasciuae faciant concede puellae
  et si quis male uir quaerit habere uirum.

Ars Amatoria I, ll. 513–524

Keep pleasantly clean, take exercise, work up an outdoor
  Tan; make quite sure that your toga fits
And doesn't show spots; don't lace your shoes too tightly
  Or ignore any rusty buckles, or slop

Around in too large a fitting. Don't let some incompetent
                                                        barber
   Ruin your looks: both hair and beard demand
Expert attention. Keep your nails pared, and dirt-free;
   Don't let those long hairs sprout
In your nostrils, make sure your breath is never offensive,
Avoid the rank male stench
   That wrinkles noses. Beyond this is for wanton women
Or any half-man who want to attract men.

                            [Peter Green]

I think we'll draw a veil over Ovid's little dig at boys who like boys. What he's going for, generally, is an approach that takes a sensible middle path between unwashed he-man and the wilder shores of David Beckham–style metrosexuality. In the passage immediately preceding this one, he warns against going over the top with the boy beauty regimen: "*sed tibi nec ferro placeat torquere capillos/nec tua mordaci pumice crura teras*" – "Don't think it's a good idea to style your hair with curling irons, or depilate your legs with stinging pumice." Ovid, it seems clear, wouldn't approve of the full back, sack and crack depilation. Where he would have stood on men's moisturising and manbags is, alas, unclear, but my sense is he would probably pour mild scorn upon them. His perfectly cogent advice is that a fellow who wants to attract the ladies should have high standards of personal hygiene, be turned out stylishly and (I think we can all raise a glass to this) definitely come minus nasal hair.

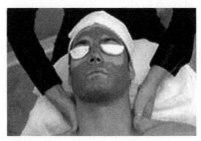

Metrosexual male . . . perhaps a step too far even for Publius Ovidius Naso

For the girls, naturally, a similar attention to detail is required. Let's have no Julia Roberts–style body hair, he advises. "*Quam paene admonui, ne trux caper iret in alas/neque forent duris aspera crura pilis*" – "I was going to advise you about grim, goaty armpits, and rough, bristling hair on your legs."

As for make-up, keep it discreet, and don't give the gentlemen any hint of all the trouble that went into the creation. Preserve some mystique.

> *non tamen expositas mensa deprendat amator*
> *pyxidas: ars faciem dissimulata iuuat.*
> *Ars Amatoria* III, ll. 209–210

But don't let your lover find all those jars and bottles

On your dressing table: the best

Make-up remains unobtrusive.

[Peter Green]

Simply emerge gorgeously "done", a creature unlike any other, as that horrible dating book *The Rules* might say. We're not interested in seeing a lump of marble, or what goes on in the artist's studio: just the beautiful finished sculpture.

Hairdos are clearly a bit of a thing for him – if only *Vogue*'s beauty pages waxed as lyrical as this:

munditiis capimur: non sint sine lege capilli;
admotae formam dantque negantque manus.
nec genus ornatus unum est: quod quamque decebit,
eligat et speculum consulat ante suum.
longa probat facies capitis discrimina puri:
sic erat ornatis Laodamia comis.
exiguum summa nodum sibi fronte relinqui,
ut pateant aures, ora rotunda uolunt.
alterius crines umero iactentur utroque:
talis es adsumpta, Phoebe canore, lyra;
altera succinctae religetur more Dianae,
ut solet, attonitas cum petit illa feras.

Ars Amatoria III, ll. 133–154

What attracts us is elegance – so don't neglect your hairstyle;
    Looks can be made or marred by a skilful touch.
Nor will one style suit all: there are innumerable fashions,
    And each girl should look in her glass
Before choosing what suits her reflection. Long features go
                         best with
  A plain central parting: that's how
Laodamia's hair was arranged. A round-faced lady
    Should pile all her hair on top,
Leaving the ears exposed. One girl should wear it down on
    Her shoulders, like Apollo about to play
The lyre; another should braid it in the style of the huntress
    Diana, when she's after some frightened beast,
Skirt hitched up.

                         [Peter Green]

Rome, the epic TV series about the last years of the Republic, gives a great sense of the complicated hairdos that were in vogue at the time. Lindsay Duncan, who plays Julius Caesar's mistress Servilia, and Polly Walker, as the hilarious Atia, mother of Octavian, are always emerging from their bedrooms with heads sporting yet more extraordinary dos topped off with elaborate curls and braids, after hours spent ensconced with their "cosmetics slaves". If you can't manage to source a fabulous wig made from the tresses of some hapless Gaulish captive, I suggest you do what Ovid says (terribly Trinny and Susannah, this): carefully pick a hairstyle that suits you. The Laodamia whom he mentions in this passage, by the way, was married to Protesilaus, the first Greek to be killed in the Trojan War, poor fellow.

The final part of the makeover is mental. Ovid suggests acquiring a smattering of Latin poetry, which, happily for you, is precisely what you're going to get if you read this book.

> *et teneri possis carmen legisse Properti*
> *siue aliquid Galli siue, Tibulle, tuum*
> *dictaque Varroni fuluis insignia uillis*
> *uellera germanae, Phrixe, querenda tuae*
> *et profugum Aenean, altae primordia Romae,*
> *quo nullum Latio clarius extat opus;*
> *forsitan et nostrum nomen miscebitur istis*
> *nec mea Lethaeis scripta dabuntur aquis*
> *atque aliquis dicet "nostri lege culta magistri*
> *carmina, quis partes instruit ille duas,*
> *deue tribus libris, titulo quos signat AMORVM,*
> *elige, quod docili molliter ore legas ..."*
>
> Ars Amatoria III, ll. 333–344

> ... Be able to quote Propertius,
> Tibullus, or Gallus, in sentimental mood;
> Learn passages from epic: the high-flown Golden

Fleece by Varro (poor Helle!), or – what else? –
Virgil's *Aeneid* (those wanderings, great Rome's origins,
    The most publicised Latin poem of all time . . .)
Perhaps, too, my own name will be included
    Among theirs, and my works escape
Oblivion: maybe some pundit will say: "Here, read our
                                        Maestro's
    Polished advice on love (for both sexes), or choose
Some pieces from the three books of his *Amores*
    To declaim in a soft, enchanting voice . . ."

                                        [Peter Green]

So cheering to see Ovid doing a bit of self-promotion on the side. Later, I'll certainly be offering you bits of Propertius and Tibullus and Virgil (and more Ovid) but, alas, the poems of Gallus and Varro did not escape oblivion, and have survived only as the merest fragments. "Poor Helle" was a character in Varro's lost translation of an epic poem in Greek called the *Argonautica*, about the Golden Fleece. She was riding on the Golden Ram as it swam over the stretch of water separating Greece from modern Turkey when she came off, and drowned – giving the Hellespont (now the Dardanelles) its name.

Gallus's poems about his girlfriend Lycoris were famous and admired by his younger contemporaries, not only Ovid but Virgil and Propertius too. He was a soldier: he fought for Octavian (the future emperor Augustus) against Mark

Antony and, after the latter's defeat at the Battle of Actium in 31 BC, was made prefect of Egypt, an extremely important job. But something went badly wrong: he was disgraced (it was perhaps that he went native, or got above himself in some way) and committed suicide in 27 BC, quite a habit of Roman grandees when faced with a public scandal.

Ovid's step two: meeting potential partners

We are not going to find a partner by sitting at home. Get out there, into the city: create opportunities to meet people. Be bold, suggests Ovid: talk to those pretty girls who are hanging out at the temple of Palatine Apollo or in Pompey's portico. And, girls, never, ever, turn down an invitation to a party:

> *sera ueni positaque decens incede lucerna:*
> *grata mora uenies, maxima lena mora est;*
> *etsi turpis eris, formosa uidebere potis,*
> *et latebras uitiis nox dabit ipsa tuis.*
> *carpe cibos digitis (est quiddam gestus edendi),*
> *ora nec immunda tota perungue manu;*
> *neue domi praesume dapes, sed desine citra*
> *quam capis: es paulo, quam potes esse, minus.*
> *Priamides Helenen auide si spectet edentem,*
> *oderit et dicat "stulta rapina mea est."*
>
> Ars Amatoria III, ll. 751–760

Arrive late, when the lamps are lit; make a
                    graceful entrance –
Delay enhances charm, delay's a great bawd.
Plain you may be, but at night you'll look fine to the tipsy:
    Soft lights and shadows will mask your faults.
Take your food with dainty fingers: good table-manners
                    matter:
    Don't besmear your whole face with a greasy paw.
Don't eat first at home, and nibble – but equally, don't
                    indulge your
    Appetite to the full, leave something in hand.
If Paris saw Helen stuffing herself to the eyeballs
    He'd detest her, he'd feel her abduction had been
A stupid mistake.   [Peter Green]

Paris, by the way, is prince of Troy. When asked by the three goddesses Minerva, Venus and Juno to pick out the most beautiful among them, he chose Venus. She rewarded him with a fabulous prize – the most beautiful woman in the world. It was spectacularly unfortunate that Helen was already married, to Menelaus, king of Sparta. When Paris ran off with her to Troy, that was the catalyst that sparked off the Greek expedition to get her back: the Trojan War.

Men, you might just want to factor in that flattering lighting when you're sizing up the girls:

hic tu fallaci nimium ne crede lucernae:
  iudicio formae noxque merumque nocent.
luce deas caeloque Paris spectauit aperto,
  cum dixit Veneri "uincis utramque, Venus."
nocte latent mendae uitioque ignoscitur omni,
  horaque formosam quamlibet illa facit.
consule de gemmis, de tincta murice lana,
  consule de facie corporibusque diem.

                                    Ars Amatoria I, ll. 245–252

    Don't trust the lamplight too much,
It's deceptive. When Paris examined those goddesses, when
                          he said, "You
    Beat them both, Venus," he did it in broad
Daylight. But darkness hides faults, each blemish is
                          forgiven:
    Any woman you name will pass
As a beauty at night. Judge jewels or fine fabrics,
    A face or a figure, *by day.*   [Peter Green]

A relief from the temple of Palatine Apollo – where Ovid
suggests you go to pick up a young lady . . .

As for actually striking up a conversation with someone you fancy? Easy, says Ovid. Here's an example. You're sitting next to a pretty girl at the races . . .

hic tibi quaeratur socii sermonis origo,
    et moueant primos publica uerba sonos:
cuius equi ueniant facito studiose requiras,
    nec mora, quisquis erit cui fauet illa, faue.
at cum pompa frequens caelestibus ibit eburnis,
    tu Veneri dominae plaude fauente manu;
utque fit, in gremium puluis si forte puellae
    deciderit, digitis excutiendus erit;
etsi nullus erit puluis, tamen excute nullum:
                                    Ars Amatoria I, ll. 143–151

    . . . Now find
some excuse to engage in friendly conversation,
    Casual small talk at first –
Ask, with a show of interest, whose are those horses
    Just coming past: find out
Her favourite, back it yourself. When the long procession of
                            ivory
    Deities approaches, be sure you give
A big hand to Lady Venus. If some dust should settle
    In your girl's lap, flick it away
With your fingers; and if there's no dust,
    Still flick away – nothing.   [Peter Green]

47

A potential seducer could give a broad hint as to his intent by enthusiastically applauding Venus, the goddess of love, when the procession of images of the gods passes. The daring might even try to cop a feel. That old flicking-away-the-dust trick, a sturdy and trusted method, even in AD 2.

Ovid's step three: continuing contact

You've made overtures to a potential lover: but how actually to embroil the target? Ovid's advice is that victory is all about self-belief. Imagine yourself invincible, and, chances are, you will be.

> *prima tuae menti ueniat fiducia, cunctas*
>   *posse capi: capies, tu modo tende plagas.*
> *uere prius uolucres taceant, aestate cicadae,*
>   *Maenalius lepori det sua terga canis,*
> *femina quam iuueni blande temptata repugnet;*
>   *haec quoque, quam poteris credere nolle, uolet.*
>   *Ars Amatoria* I, ll. 269–274

The first thing to get in your head is that every single
    Girl can be caught – and that you'll catch her if
You set your toils right. Birds will sooner fall dumb in
                           spring time,
    Cicadas in summer, or a hunting-dog

Turn his back on a hare, than a lover's bland inducements
   Can fail with a woman.

[Peter Green]

Not actually true in the real world, gentlemen. But the point is: be bold, be resolute and, if you expect success, you will be pretty likely to meet with it.

Keeping in touch with a new love interest requires special skill. Ovid may have been talking about letters written on wax tablets, but exactly the same applies to e-mail. Used carefully, correspondence can be a great part of your battery. Used badly, it can scupper your chances. Don't be too high falutin' in your writing style: it should be clear and conversational. "*Sit tibi credibilis sermo consuetaque uerba,/blanda tamen, praesens ut uideare loqui*" – "use eve ryday language, familiar yet flattering words, as though you were there, in her presence."

On the other hand, write carefully. Illiterate communications are a major turn-off. Ovid, quite rightly, warns against a "*barbara lingua*", "a barbarous style". I am going to take a giant leap and suggest that this includes the use of all emoticons in electronic communications. People, don't. And don't reply absolutely at once. You don't want to look desperate, do you? "*Postque breuem rescribe moram: mora semper amantes incitat*" – "Write back after a little delay: delay always fires up lovers," says Ovid.

By this time, if you have followed all the poet's steps faithfully, you should have pulled! And if not, keep trying. Persistence is everything. He re, he's talking about the famously faithful Penelope. While her husband Odysseus was away fighting the Trojan War for ten years, and then for another decade trying to make it home to Ithaca across the Mediterranean, she was assailed by suitors trying to get her to marry them.

> *quid magis est saxo durum, quid mollius unda?*
> *dura tamen molli saxa cauantur aqua.*
> *Penelopen ipsam, persta modo, tempore uinces:*
> *capta uides sero Pergama, capta tamen.*
>
> *Ars Amatoria* I, ll. 475–478

> What is softer than water,
> What harder than stone? Yet the soft
> Water-drip hollows hard rock. In time, with persistence,
> You'll conquer Penelope. Troy fell late,
> But fall it did.
>
> [Peter Green]

Remember: Rome wasn't built in a day.

III. LOVED UP

mi neque amare aliam neque ab hac desistere fas est:
Cynthia prima fuit, Cynthia finis erit
It's my fate never to love another nor to abandon her.
Cynthia was the first. Cynthia will be the end.
Propertius, I.12

When you're in love, it's the two of you against the world. Think Romeo and Juliet, Bonnie and Clyde, Tristan and Isolde. That's the sentiment that floods out of Catullus's Poem Five, with which we ended the first chapter:

Viuamus, mea Lesbia, atque amemus
rumoresque senum seueriorum
omnes unius aestimemus assis.

ll. 1–3

My Lesbia, let us live and love
And not care tuppence for old men
Who sermonise and disapprove.   [James Michie]

Lovers are elsewhere, in a sphere apart: in Edith Wharton's *The Age of Innocence*, when Madame Olenska and Newland Archer take the steamboat together in Boston, the last gasp of their impossible love, "it seemed to Archer that everything in the old familiar world of habit was receding also . . . now that she was beside him, and they were drifting forth into this unknown world, they seemed to have reached the kind of deeper nearness that a touch may sunder."

In John Donne's wonderful poem "The Sun Rising", where the poet chides the "busy old fool, unruly Sun" for breaking off the night of pleasure he has been enjoying with his mistress, he puts the feeling this way:

> She's all states, and all princes I;
> Nothing else is;
> Princes do but play us; compared to this,
> All honour's mimic, all wealth alchemy.

Being loved up means you want to shout your happiness from the rooftops – this from the poet Sulpicia:

> *Tandem uenit amor qualem texisse pudore*
> *quam nudasse alicui sit mihi fama magis.*
> *exorata meis illum Cytherea Camenis*
> *attulit in nostrum deposuitque sinum.*
> *exsoluit promissa Venus. mea gaudia narret*
> *dicetur si quis non habuisse sua.*
> *non ego signatis quicquam mandare tabellis*
> *ne legat id nemo quam meus ante, uelim.*
> *sed peccasse iuuat, uultus componere famae*
> *taedet. cum digno digna fuisse ferar.*

At last has come a love which it would disgrace me more
To hide out of shame than expose to someone.
Prevailed upon by my Camenae, Cytherea
Delivered him into my arms on trust.
Venus has kept her promise. My joys can be the talk
Of all who are said to have none of their own.
I would not wish to send a message under seal
So no one could read it before my man.
But I'm glad to sin and tired of wearing reputation's
Mask. The world shall know I've met my match.

[Guy Lee]

The Camenae – catchily named Carmenta, Egeria, Antevorta and Postvorta – were Roman goddesses, spirits of springs and fountains. They were sometimes associated with the Greek Muses. And Cytherea is a name for Venus, goddess of love. So perhaps there's a hint that it was Sulpicia's creative inspiration, her poetry itself, that brought her love to her. Here is the poem again given a romantic, eighteenth-century makeover by George, Lord Lyttelton, published after his death in 1774. (It doesn't seem terribly likely to me that Sulpicia herself would have gone with all that stuff about woman's weakness for man, but never mind.)

I'm weary of this tedious dull deceit;
Myself I torture, while the world I cheat.

Tho' Prudence bids me strive to guard my flame,
Love sees the low hypocrisy with shame;
Love bids me all confess and call thee mine,
Worthy my heart, as I am worthy thine:
Weakness for thee I will no longer hide;
Weakness for thee is woman's noblest pride.

Six short and beautiful poems by this Sulpicia are the only poems written by a woman in ancient Rome that now survive. She was, it's thought, a niece of Augustus's general Messalla, who was a great patron of poets including Tibullus. In fact Sulpicia's tiny oeuvre – probably written in the 20s BC, the first decade of Augustus's reign – came down to us with Tibullus's poems, and was once attributed to him.

Loved up also means the object of your passion shines more brightly than anyone else in the world. You have eyes only for them; they are different, godlike. No one else, even if they have the good looks of an Achilles or a Helen, is on the radar. Catullus in Poem 86 tries to get to the bottom of what makes his adored Lesbia different from the perfectly lovely Quintia:

Quintia formosa est multis; mihi candida, longa,
*   recta est. haec ego sic singula confiteor.*
totum illud "formosa" nego. nam nulla uenustas,
*   nulla in tam magno est corpore mica salis.*
Lesbia formosa est, quae cum pulcerrima tota est,
*   tum omnibus una omnis surripuit ueneres.*

Quintia is beautiful, many will tell you: to me
She is white, she is straight, she is tall: to all this
                    I agree,
But does this make her beautiful? though she be
                    found without fault,
Can you find in the whole of her body the
                    least pinch of salt?
But Lesbia is beautiful, hers is the secret alone
To steal from all beauty its beauty, and make it her
                    own.

                              [Arthur Symons]

The lover's body – we adore it, anatomise it, fetishise it, glory in it, want to possess it, even to disappear into it: "intimately to mix and melt and to be melted together with his beloved, so that one should be made out of two" (that's Shelley translating Plato's *Symposium*, the ancient Greek philosophical dialogue on the nature of love). Catullus's Poem Two is a schoolroom favourite – in which the poet watches Lesbia play with her pet sparrow, a sight clearly as riveting for Catullus as was Charlotte cutting slices of bread-and-butter for Goethe's Werther:

Passer, deliciae meae puellae,
quicum ludere, quem in sinu tenere,

cui primum digitum dare appetenti
et acris solet incitare morsus
cum desiderio meo nitenti
carum nescio quid lubet iocari
et solaciolum sui doloris,
credo, ut tum grauis acquiescat ardor:
tecum ludere sicut ipsa possem
et tristis animi leuare curas!

Sparrow, my Lesbia's darling pet,
Her playmate whom she loves to let
Perch in her bosom and then tease
With tantalising fingertips,
Provoking angry little nips
(For my bright beauty seems to get
A kind of pleasure from these games,
Even relief, this being her way,
I think, of damping down the flames
Of passion), I wish I could play
Silly games with you, too, to ease
My worries and my miseries.

[James Michie]

All that nipping and teasing – it's erotic and highly charged. I think he'd rather be playing with Lesbia than playing with her sparrow. And I think he's just a bit jealous of it.

There's an extraordinary passage in Proust's *The Captive*, when Marcel, the narrator of *A la Recherche du temps perdu*, describes his loved one, Albertine, asleep:

> "By shutting her eyes, by losing consciousness, Albertine had stripped off, one after another, the different human personalities with which she had deceived me ever since the day when I had first made her acquaintance. She was animated now only by the unconscious life of plants, of trees, a life more different from my own, more alien, and yet one that belonged more to me. Her personality was not constantly escaping, as when we talked, by the outlets of her unacknowledged thoughts and of her eyes. She had called back into herself everything of her that lay outside, had withdrawn, enclosed, reabsorbed, in her body. In keeping it in front of my eyes, in my hands, I had that impression of possessing her entirely, which I never had when she was awake. Her life was submitted to me, exhaled towards me its gentle breath."
>
> [CK Scott Moncrieff and Terence Kilmartin]

Of all the Latin love poets, Propertius is the one who comes closest to Proust in the way he attempts, over and over again, to express what being in love actually feels like. In fact I think Propertius is a poet whose work it's good to try to read as a whole rather than piecemeal. He covers the same territory repeatedly, almost relentlessly, holding love up to the light and examining it from every angle, such that some of his poetry's effect comes from the way it layers and accretes in your mind after a time. He uses lots of mythology: an old story will often do more for him, spark off more richly suggestive associations, than bald statements about something that is as fugitive, and essentially language-resistant, as love. His poems often start in one place and in one tone, and end up inhabiting an entirely different mood. Cynthia, the subject of these obsessive poems, is at once his adored goddess and a tyrannical, domineering mistress. There are poems in which he describes himself as her slave – an extraordinarily transgressive, emasculating notion in a society that regarded slaves as barely human. Yet he's a willing one too – he talks of his "*dulcia uincla*", "sweet chains", in his Poem Three.

Anyway, that's all by way of introduction. Here, like Marcel gazing at Albertine, the poet watches Cynthia as she sleeps. Unlike the valetudinarian Marcel (whom I've never quite forgiven for having been made ill by two cups of tea), he's drunk. This is a long poem, but it's worth quoting in full, because it ends up in such a different place from where it began.

Qualis Thesea iacuit cedente carina
   languida desertis Cnosia litoribus;
qualis et accubuit primo Cepheia somno
   libera iam duris cotibus Andromede;
nec minus assiduis Edonis fessa choreis

qualis in herboso concidit Apidano:
talis uisa mihi mollem spirare quietem
    Cynthia non certis nixa caput manibus,
ebria cum multo traherem uestigia Baccho,
    et quaterent sera nocte facem pueri.
hanc ego, nondum etiam sensus deperditus omnis,
    molliter impresso conor adire toro;
et quamuis duplici correptum ardore iuberent
    hac Amor hac Liber, durus uterque deus,
subiecto leuiter positam temptare lacerto
    osculaque admota sumere et arma manu,
non tamen ausus eram dominae turbare quietem,
    expertae metuens iurgia saeuitiae:
sed sic intentis haerebam fixus ocellis,
    Argus ut ignotis cornibus Inachidos.
et modo gaudebam lapsos formare capillos;
    nunc furtiua cauis poma dabam manibus;
omniaque ingrato largibar munera somno,
    munera de prono saepe uoluta sinu;
et quotiens raro duxit suspiria motu,
    obstupui uano credulus auspicio,
ne qua tibi insolitos portarent uisa timores,
    neue quis inuitam cogeret esse suam:
donec diuersas praecurrens luna fenestras,
    luna moraturis sedula luminibus,
compositos leuibus radiis patefecit ocellos.
    sic ait in molli fixa toro cubitum:

"tandem te nostro referens iniuria lecto
    alterius clausis expulit e foribus?
namque ubi longa meae consumpsti tempora noctis,
    languidus exactis, ei mihi, sideribus?
o utinam talis perducas, improbe, noctes,
    me miseram qualis semper habere iubes!
nam modo purpureo fallebam stamine somnum,
    rursus et Orpheae carmine, fessa, lyrae;
interdum leuiter mecum deserta querebar
    externo longas saepe in amore moras:
dum me iucundis lapsam sopor impulit alis.
    illa fuit lacrimis ultima cura meis."

As on the lonely beach the Cnossian lay
Fainting while Theseus' keel receded;
As Cepheus' Andromeda, free at last
From the rocks, reclined in her first sleep;
As one exhausted in the Thracian
Ring-dance falls in a heap on Apidanus' sward;
Just so, it seemed to me, did Cynthia breathe
Soft quietude, head propped on outspread hands,
When deep in wine I dragged my footsteps in
As the slaves shook up the late-night torches.

I, not yet quite totally deprived of all my senses,
Endeavoured softly to go to her dinted bed –
Although here Love, here Wine, each god strong

As the other, ordered me, goaded with double fire,
Lightly to pass my arm beneath her prostrate form
And seize and hold her, venturing kisses.

Yet, fearing the furious objurgations I knew so well,
I did not dare disturb my mistress' peace:
Fast I stood, with riveted eyes, like Argus
Before Inachus' daughter's strange horns.
Now I untied the garland from my head,
And put it, Cynthia, about your brows.
And now I joyed to arrange your straying locks,
And covertly place apples in your hands:
But I lavished all my gifts on thankless sleep –
The gifts that rolled profuse from my leaning breast!

And when you stirred at times and heaved a sigh,
I stood transfixed with empty apprehension
Lest visions brought you unaccustomed dread
And someone strove to make you, unwilling, his:
But then the moon, fleeting past the open shutters,
The officious moon, whose light would linger,
Opened with gentle beams your eyes becalmed.

Her elbow propped in the soft bed, then she said:
"Has another's 'injustice' chased you out and shut
The doors and brought you back, at last, to me?

Where have you squandered the watches of my night,
And droop (alas for me) now the stars are put out?
If only you might endure, you shameless man,

         such nights

As you always enforce on my misfortune!

I have eluded sleep with nitid weaving,
And then, worn out, with a song to Orpheus' lyre,
Lamented quietly in my loneliness
Your frequent long delays in love with strangers,
Until Oblivion brushed my sinking form
With his welcome wings. And that
Was my latest concern, amid my tears."

          [WG Shepherd]

I told you Propertius used mythology a lot, and this poem is no exception. Here's a quick crib: The Cnossian is Ariadne, who helped Theseus defeat the Cretan minotaur. (Knossos, which you can visit today, it having been excavated and "imaginatively" restored by Arthur Evans, was the royal palace.) Andromeda was the girl who was rescued from a sea-monster by Perseus, the hero who rode the winged horse Pegasus and brandished the Gorgon's head to turn people to stone. (Perseus petrified, and I mean literally, Andromeda's dad, Cepheus, when he refused to let him and Andromeda marry.) The Thracian ring-dance – that's a reference to the orgiastic, sacred rites of Dionysus which involved night-long dancing. And the Apidanus is a river in Thessaly.

As I was saying: loved up, we create a phantom of the object of our desires, a creature who, for better or worse, may have little to do with the real living, breathing person. Here

Waiting for love ... Marcel Proust

Propertius has come home late, slightly the worse for wear. Like Albertine, who is also a bit of a tricky wicket, asleep is one place where Cynthia can't argue. At peace, and tranquil, she can be made into whatever Propertius wants her to be. (It makes me think a little of Pygmalion, who sculpted his ideal girl out of stone and brought her alive.) And so he fantasises that she's these glorious creatures of myth. He goes on: "Fast I stood, with riveted eyes, like Argus/Before Inachus' daughter's strange horns." Inachus's daughter was Io, who was turned into a heifer by Juno out of jealousy, because Jupiter had taken a shine to her. Juno also sent a bodyguard to keep watch on Io: the giant Argus, who had a hundred eyes. So it's slightly joky, this: Propertius is entranced by Cynthia, drinking her in as if he had a hundred eyes. As Proust wrote: "In keeping [her] in front of my eyes, in my hands, I had that impression of possessing her entirely, which I never had when she was awake."

However, Cynthia does wake up. A moonbeam passes over her face and disturbs her. The wakeful Cynthia is no mythical heroine, but a very modern Roman girl who's rather put out: she waited up half the night for Propertius, keeping herself awake by playing her lyre and weaving (that's a veiled reference to Penelope, the faithful wife of Odysseus, who worked at the loom while he was off fighting the Trojan War). Finally she gave up and dropped off to sleep, only to be woken again by her drunken boyfriend. It's very affectionate, this picture of the irritated Cynthia, who reckons Propertius must have been out with another woman. But mythical heroine, perhaps thankfully, she ain't: she's certainly all-too real.

Catullus's Poem 68 is another poem that hums with myth. It's a curious, rich and experimental thing, 160 lines long, dedicated to someone called Allius, thanking him for the loan of a house where the poet and Lesbia met to make love. It is, partly, about that feeling of light-headed, glorious anticipation, of waiting for a lover to appear at a rendezvous – a moment that is a little tinged with melancholy. It's totally different in some ways, but it does remind me of that bit in Nancy Mitford's *The Pursuit of Love* when Linda is waiting for her lover Fabrice to arrive at her house by the Thames in Chelsea. (Linda seems to do more waiting around than anyone else in English literature, first as a teenager as she waits for love to strike; then as she endlessly waits for Fabrice to come back from the war; and finally as she waits for her baby to be born.)

"The Sunday silence was broken by two swans swinging slowly upstream, and then by the chugging of a little barge, while she waited for that other sound, a sound more intimately connected with the urban love affair than any except the telephone-bell, that of a stopping taxicab... Presently she heard it in the street, slowly, slower, it stopped, the flag went up with a ring, the door slammed, voices, clinking coins, footsteps."

Here's Catullus waiting for Lesbia chez Allius:

is clausum lato patefecit limite campum,
isque domum nobis isque dedit dominae,
ad quam communes exerceremus amores,
quo mea se molli candida diua pede
intulit et trito fulgentem in limine plantam

innixa arguta constituit solea,
coniugis ut quondam flagrans aduenit amore
Protesilaëam Laodamia domum
inceptam frustra, nondum cum sanguine sacro
hostia caelestis pacificasset eros.

l. 67–76

He opened a fenced field with a broad bridle-path,
He gave me and my mistress a house,
Under whose roof we could engage in shared love,
Where my radiant goddess with soft step
Drew near and rested a dazzling foot on the worn sill,
Pressing it with creaking sandal,
As in the past, ablaze with love for a husband, came
Laodamia to the house Protesilaus
Began in vain because no victim's sacred blood
Had yet appeased the Lords of Heaven.

[Guy Lee]

In Catullus's lines, everything is heightened; you can feel the force of his expectation. When Lesbia does come in, it's a wonderfully cinematic moment. You can see that delicious white foot – in close-up – contrasting with the worn, rough-hewn stone of the doorstep. I think of Catullus as waiting for Lesbia in the next room; for me, he's imagining the sight of her as he hears her footstep and the noise her leather sandal makes.

Alas, the apparently distant real world has a way of bursting rudely into private happiness. Catullus compares Lesbia to the mythical Laodamia, stepping into her beloved husband's home on her wedding day. It's not a propitious parallel: there had been no sacrifice to the gods before that ceremony: rather an unfortunate oversight, since it led to Protesilaus being the first of the Greeks to be killed during the Trojan War.

But let's not end on that gloomy intrusion, rather on Catullus in full loved-up bliss – Poem Seven. Another crib needed here: Battus was the mythical founder of Cyrene in Libya, which was famous for silphium, a herb. And the famous oracle of Jupiter Ammon was at the Saharan oasis of Siwa. Oh, and Catullus is completely insatiable. He just can't get enough.

Quaeris, quot mihi basiationes
tuae, Lesbia, sint satis superque.
quam magnus numerus Libyssae harenae
lasarpiciferis iacet Cyrenis
oraclum Iouis inter aestuosi
et Batti ueteris sacrum sepulcrum;
aut quam sidera multa, cum tacet nox,
furtiuos hominum uident amores:
tam te basia multa basiare
uesano satis et super Catullo est

quae nec pernumerare curiosi
possint nec mala fascinare lingua.

How many kisses satisfy,
How many are enough and more,
You ask me, Lesbia. I reply,
As many as the Libyan sands
Sprinkling the Cyrenaic shore
Where silphium grows, between the places
Where old King Battus's tomb stands
And Jupiter Ammon has his shrine
In Siwa's sweltering oasis;
As many as the stars above
That in the dead of midnight shine
Upon men's secrecies of love.
When he has all those kisses, mad-
Hungry Catullus will have had
Enough to slake his appetite –
So many that sharp eyes can't tell
The number, and the tongues of spite
Are too confused to form a spell.

[James Michie]

IV. HOW TO KEEP THEM

ut ameris, amabilis esto
If you want to be loved, be lovable
Ovid, *Ars Amatoria* II

O nce you've pulled in your target, how do you make sure that she or he is not going to slip through your fingers? How are you going to ensure your new lover's continued and long-term enthusiasm for wonderful, wonderful you? There's no point reeling in a fabulous lover only to wake up next to a note on the pillow (I'm thinking of poor old Carrie in *Sex and the City*, dumped by Post-it note by that rat Berger, not at all satisfactory).

I'm afraid at this juncture, you're going to have to put in a lot of legwork. Like Ovid says: "*Amor odit inertes*" – "love hates shirkers". Were I the writer of a proper self-help book, I would advise you to repeat this phrase in a self-motivational style in front of a mirror. The other phrase of Ovid's you could usefully be intoning is "*militat omnis amans*" – "every lover is a soldier", or every lover is on active service. That comes from his *Amores*, Book One, Poem Nine, in which he wittily – and, frankly, subversively – compares the proper Roman work of going out and conquering the world by force of arms to the lazy and unproductive business (or so conventional Roman thought would have it) of making love.

A lover and a soldier are alike, he teases, because each has to be fit and healthy, each has to lay siege effectively (to cities, or, as it might be, girls' houses); each has to be in training for (hem hem), night exercises.

Make love, not war – it's definitely worth it in Asterix . . .

My point is this: the life of love might look like it's all about reclining on couches while topless slave girls, or boys, feed you peeled grapes, but, according to Ovid, you gotta work at it. Making love, he implies, is its own kind of "*negotium*" – the word the Romans used for businesslike getting-on-with-things. So, get into the habit. Plan this relationship with military precision. Put some effort into being attentive to the adored one. Laugh at their jokes. Flatter them. Show them that you're just fascinated by eve rything they have to say. If you're playing Scrabble with them, be sure they win. Do lovely little tasks for them. Gentlemen, be chivalrous:

> arguet: arguito; quicquid probat illa, probato;
>> quod dicet, dicas; quod negat illa, neges.
> riserit: adride; si flebit, flere memento:
>> imponat leges uultibus illa tuis.
> seu ludet numerosque manu iactabit eburnos,
>> tu male iactato, tu male iacta dato . . .
> ipse tene distenta suis umbracula uirgis,
>> ipse fac in turba, qua uenit illa, locum.
> nec dubita tereti scamnum producere lecto,
>> et tenero soleam deme uel adde pedi.
> saepe etiam dominae, quamuis horrebis et ipse,
>> algenti manus est calficienda sinu.
>>>> *Ars Amatoria* II, ll. 199–204; 209–214

Censure the things she censures,
Endorse her endorsements, echo her every word,
Pro or con, and laugh whenever she laughs; remember,
If she weeps, to weep too: take your cue
From her every expression. Suppose she's playing a board
game,

Then throw the dice carelessly, move
Your pieces all wrong. At knucklebones, when you beat her,
    Exact no forfeit, roll low throws yourself
As often as you can manage. If you're playing halma, permit
                                    her
    Glass piece to take yours. Open up
Her parasol, hold it over her when she's out walking,
    Clear her a path through the crowd.
When she's on her chaise-longue, make haste to find a
                                    footstool
    For those dainty feet of hers, help her on and off
With her slippers. At times she'll feel cold: then (though
                                    you're shivering
    Yourself) warm her tiny hand
In your bosom.

                                    [Peter Green]

It's all about gazing deeply into the eyes of the object of
your desire, and making them feel as if they are the centre of
the very universe. Their tiny hand is frozen? Be sure to hold
it in your own, as I am sure Puccini would also advise. Subtly
communicate the notion that their conversation alternates
between the uttermost profundities and the gayest, brightest
wit. (By the way, the next time a man finds me a footstool
while I am lying on my chaise-longue I will be lobbying to
create a national holiday in celebration. I submit that any

Never underestimate the effects of a chaise-longue – wise advice from Ovid

man who does this for a woman is guaranteed luck in love for ever.)

Here's something very easily forgotten by men: remember to compliment a lady on her outfit. It's an easy-peasy way into a girl's good books. And as Ovid implies, just do it, whether or not you're a particular fan of the ensemble in question. "*Siue erit in Tyriis, Tyrios laudabis amictus;/siue erit in Cois, Coa decere puta./aurata est: ipso tibi sit pretiosior auro*" – "If she's in purple, praise purple; if she's in Coan silk, say Coan silk suits her. If she's in gold, say she's more precious than gold."

You could also try showing your beloved how much you care with some creative work (though the recipient might well prefer an expensive present, admits Ovid with feeling):

sunt tamen et doctae, rarissima turba, puellae,
altera non doctae turba, sed esse uolunt.
utraque laudetur per carmina; carmina lector
commendet dulci qualiacumque sono.
his ergo aut illis uigilatum carmen in ipsas
forsitan exigui muneris instar erit.

Ars Amatoria II, ll. 281–286

There *are* a few cultured girls (not many, it's true), and others
Who'd like to be cultured, but aren't;
Flatter any of these with poems: a bravura declamation
Even of trash – this will suffice to win
Their approval. Clever or stupid, they'll take a poem
fashioned
In the small hours, for *them*, as a cute little gift.

[Peter Green]

I'm not sure I'm with the great P. Ovidius Naso on this one – most girls in my experience have enough discernment and are sufficiently "*doctae*", or "cultured", not to go all mushy about a bloke just because he's written some doggerel for her, and in some cases I've known it be completely counter-productive.

Next is a most important point: if you want to be in this relationship for the long haul, you can't rely on good looks:

74

... ut ameris, amabilis esto;
quod tibi non facies solaue forma dabit.
sic licet antiquo Nireus adamatus Homero
Naiadumueque tener crimine raptus Hylas,
ut dominam teneas nec te mirere relictum,
ingenii dotes corporis adde bonis . . .
nec leuis ingenuas pectus coluisse per artes
cura sit et linguas edidicisse duas:
non formosus erat, sed erat facundus Ulixes,
et tamen aequoreas torsit amore deas.

Ars Amatoria II, ll.107–112; 121–124

To be loved you must show yourself lovable –
Something good looks alone
Can never achieve. You may be handsome as Homer's
Nireus,
Or young Hylas, snatched by those bad
Naiads; but all the same, to avoid a surprise desertion
And keep your girl, it's best you have gifts of mind
In addition to physical charms . . .
... Keep your wits sharp, explore the liberal
Arts, win a mastery over Greek
As well as Latin. Ulysses was eloquent, not handsome –
Yet he filled sea-goddesses' hearts
With aching passion.   [Peter Green]

Funnily enough, that's true, I think. In the famous classicists' parlour game (that I have just this minute invented) called Which Character from Classical Myth Would You Most Like to Date, my answer would be Odysseus. He was clever, resourceful, witty, told a good story ... admittedly he wasn't absolutely 100 per cent faithful to Penelope; on his ten-year journey back to home after the Trojan War he had lengthy affairs with the witch Circe and the nymph Calypso, the sea goddesses mentioned here, but there again he did make good in the end, what with his coming home and killing all those suitors who'd been hassling Penelope for years. And at least he'd got a bit more going for him than Achilles, who was a moody, self-important sod (if gorgeous; he was Brad Pitt in the film *Troy* if you'll remember).

Beautiful Ithaca, home of Odysseus, winner of the parlour game,
Which Character from Classical Myth Would You Most Like to Date

Ovid has a bit of special-interest know-how for those who are involved with someone who really ought to be off-limits. In his collection of love poems, the *Amores*, Book One, Poem Four, he encourages his mistress to communicate with him in code when they meet in company – she's with her "official" escort:

cum tibi succurret Veneris lasciuia nostrae,
*   purpureas tenero pollice tange genas;*
si quid erit, de me tacita quod mente queraris,
*   pendeat extrema mollis ab aure manus;*
cum tibi, quae faciam, mea lux, dicamue, placebunt,
*   uersetur digitis anulus usque tuis;*
tange manu mensam, tangunt quo more precantes,
*   optabis merito cum mala multa uiro.*
quod tibi miscuerit, sapias, bibat ipse iubeto;
*   tu puerum leuiter posce, quod ipsa uoles:*
quae tu reddideris, ego primus pocula sumam,
*   et, qua tu biberis, hac ego parte bibam.*
si tibi forte dabit quod praegustauerit ipse,
*   reice libatos illius ore cibos;*
nec premat impositis sinito tua colla lacertis,
*   mite nec in rigido pectore pone caput,*
nec sinus admittat digitos habilesue papillae;
*   oscula praecipue nulla dedisse uelis.*
oscula si dederis, fiam manifestus amator

et dicam "mea sunt" iniciamque manum.
haec tamen aspiciam, sed quae bene pallia celant,
  illa mihi caeci causa timoris erunt.
nec femori committe femur nec crure cohaere
  nec tenerum duro cum pede iunge pedem.
multa miser timeo, quia feci multa proterue,
  exemplique metu torqueor ipse mei:
saepe mihi dominaeque meae properata uoluptas
  ueste sub iniecta dulce peregit opus.

Amores I.4, ll. 21–48

When you're thinking about the last time we made love
                                together,
  Touch your rosy cheek with one elegant thumb.
If you're cross with me, and can't say so, then pinch the
                                bottom
  Of your earlobe. But when I do or say
Something that gives you especial pleasure, my darling,
  Keep turning the ring on your finger to and fro,
When you yearn for your man to suffer some well-merited
                                misfortune
  Place your hands on the table as though in prayer.
If he mixes wine specially for you, watch out, make him
                                drink it

Himself. Ask the waiter for what *you* want
As you hand back the goblet. I'll be the first to seize it
    And drink from the place your lips have touched.
If *he* offers you tit-bits out of some dish he's tasted,
    Refuse what's been near his mouth.
Don't let him put his arms round your neck, and oh, don't
                                            lay that
        Darling head of yours on *his* coarse breast.
Don't let his fingers roam down your dress to touch up
    Those responsive nipples. Above all, don't you dare
Kiss him, not once. If you do, I'll proclaim myself your
                                            lover,
        Lay hand upon you, claim those kisses as mine.
So much for what I can see. But there's plenty goes on
                                            under
    A long evening wrap. The mere thought worries me
                                            stiff.
Don't start rubbing your thigh against his, don't go playing
    Footsy under the table, keep smooth from rough.
(I'm scared all right, and no wonder – I've been too
                                            successful
    An operator myself, it's my own
Example I find so unnerving. I've often petted to climax
    With my darling at a party, hand hidden under her cloak.
                                            [Peter Green]

Sorry about the slightly queasy-making "petted to climax" in this translation. One might prefer Christopher Marlowe's "I and my wench oft under clothes did lurke,/When pleasure mov'd us to our sweetest worke." (He also has the line, from this passage, "Thy bosomes Roseat buds let him not finger", which is strangely memorable.)

Finally, Ovid's top tip. If you've had a row, if you've been at each other's throats, what you want is a really good bout of make-up sex:

cum bene saeuierit, cum certa uidebitur hostis,
　　tum pete concubitus foedera: mitis erit.
illic depositis habitat Concordia telis,
　　illo, crede mihi, Gratia nata loco est.
quae modo pugnarunt, iungunt sua rostra columbae,
　　quarum blanditias uerbaque murmur habet.

Ars Amatoria II, l. 461–466

When she's been raging at you, when she seems utterly
　　　　　　　　　　　　　　　　　　hostile,
　　Then is the time to try
An alliance in bed. She'll come through. Bed's where
　　　　　　　　　　　　　　harmony dwells when
　　The fighting's done: that's the place

Where loving-kindness was born. The doves that
                           lately fought now
    Call softly, bill and coo.

                                           [Peter Green]

It's tough work, love, but somebody's got to do it.
"*Militat omnis amans . . .*"

V. DUMPED

"Num lacrimas victus dedit aut miseratus amantem est?"
Has he softened, or shed a tear for someone who loved him?
Virgil, *Aeneid* IV

There's probably no good way to break up with someone. Still, there are surely certain standards to be upheld. Such as having the grace to do it kindly, in person; and using one's God-given powers of empathy to show some respect and kindness to your dumpee. You certainly shouldn't dump someone on TV, like Matt Damon did. You definitely shouldn't dump your girlfriend while she is pregnant, like Daniel Day-Lewis did. And you should be taken out and shot for dumping someone by Post-it note, like Berger did. (OK, the last one is in an episode from *Sex and the City* that I've already mentioned, and not actually real, but you can see where I'm going with this. I'd also like to enquire, in parenthesis, whether we think it's coincidence that the aforementioned love rats are all men.) Virgil, arguably the greatest Roman poet of them all, provided a brilliant object lesson in how not to break up with a girlfriend in his wonderful epic poem, the *Aeneid* – and it still holds good today.

The *Aeneid* was drafted but not revised by the time its author died in 19 BC. He left instructions for it to be destroyed, but thank God, and I say this even as someone who battled with the wretched thing at school and university, he was completely ignored by his friend and fellow poet Lucius Varius Rufus, who arranged for it to be published posthumously. It's the richest and most important piece of literature produced in ancient Rome, telling the story of the Trojan prince Aeneas and his companions: they bale out of the sacked city after the Greeks win the war, have *Odyssey*-style adventures as they sail through the Mediterranean, and finally end up in Italy, where his descendent Romulus will, generations later, establish the eternal city. It's Rome's foundation myth–cum–national epic – but far too rich and dense and full of ambiguities to be simply national propaganda, even though Virgil's patron was Maecenas, the emperor Augustus's close friend and the most important patron of the arts in Rome.

Early in the poem, en route to Italy, the Trojans find themselves in Carthage, on the coast of modern Tunisia, where the fabulous, beautiful, stylish and entirely capable Queen Dido is founding a new nation. Aeneas and Dido fall in love, with a bit of help from the interfering Venus (Aeneas's mother, goddess of love) and Juno (wife of Jupiter, king of the gods). They get it together in adventurously *al fresco* fashion, in a cave, while sheltering from a rainstorm during a hunt. But pretty quickly the gods realise that unless

Aeneas shifts himself out of Africa, he'll never reach Italy, meaning Rome will never be founded. That, of course, will never do – no Roman empire, no scary world domination, no Latin poetry, no underfloor heating, no straight roads, etc., etc. So they send a messenger, Mercury, to chivvy Aeneas along.

This precipitates one of the most disastrously managed break-ups in history. (And this bit of the *Aeneid*, Book Four, is spectacularly good, one of the finest pieces of writing ever produced, inspiring, into the bargain, two extraordinary operas in Purcell's *Dido and Aeneas* and Berlioz's *Les Troyens*.)

Sing along with Dido and Aeneas . . .

Aeneas, you see, behaves like a worm. Instead of confronting Dido and calmly but kindly telling her that he's been called abruptly away to lay the foundations of the world's greatest empire, he bottles out. He chats to his useless male friends (almost always an idiotic idea), and decides that it's best they all start packing; he'll choose a moment "at the right time" to tell Dido he's sacking her.

Because she's not entirely stupid, she senses what's going on, and is very cross indeed. For if there is one thing worse than being dumped, it's knowing that someone is about to dump you, and has talked it over with their no doubt detestable mates, but just hasn't got the courage to spit it out.

> *. . . eadem impia Fama furenti*
> *detulit armari classem cursumque parari.*
> *saeuit inops animi totamque incensa per urbem*
> *bacchatur, qualis commotis excita sacris*
> *Thyias, ubi audito stimulant trieterica Baccho*
> *orgia nocturnusque uocat clamore Cithaeron.*
> *tandem his Aenean compellat uocibus ultro:*
> *"dissimulare etiam sperasti, perfide, tantum*
> *posse nefas tacitusque mea decedere terra?*
> *nec te noster amore nec te data dextera quondam*
> *nec moritura tenet crudeli funere Dido?*
>
> Aeneid IV, ll. 298–308

> . . . Rumour, vicious as ever,
> brings her word, already distraught, that Trojans
> are rigging out their galleys, gearing to set sail.

She rages in helpless frenzy, blazing through
the entire city, raving like some Maenad
driven wild when the women shake the sacred emblems,
when the cyclic orgy, shouts of "Bacchus" fire her on
and Cithaeron echoes round with maddened midnight cries.

At last she assails Aeneas, before he's said a word:
"So, you traitor, you really believed you'd keep
this a secret, this great outrage? Steal away
in silence from my shores? Can nothing hold you back?
Not our love? Not the pledge once sealed with our right
hands?
Not even the thought of Dido doomed to a cruel death?
[Robert Fagles]

In other words, Dido gets weepy and shouty; and, gentlemen, though she may have overreacted just the teeniest bit, what with the running riot round Carthage as if in a Bacchanalian frenzy, I am not altogether sure I can blame her. Clearly, this is no way for a man to behave.

Having been thus confronted by Dido, Aeneas then makes a totally inadequate and tactless speech: if he'd had his own way he'd still be in Troy rather than this poor excuse for a city; it's not about her, it's about him and the gods' commands. I am sure we all know the sort of thing only too well.

"ego te, quae plurima fando
enumerare uales, numquam, regina, negabo
promeritam, nec me meminisse pigebit Elissae
dum memor ipse mei, dum spiritus hos regit artus.
pro re pauca loquar. neque ego hanc abscondere furto
speraui (ne finge) fugam, nec coniugis umquam
praetendi taedas aut haec in foedera ueni.
me si fata meis paterentur ducere uitam
auspiciis et sponte mea componere curas,
urbem Troianam primum dulcisque meorum
reliquias colerem, Priami tecta alta manerent,
et recidiua manu posuissem Pergama uictis.
sed nunc Italiam magnam Grynneus Apollo,
Italiam Lyciae iussere capessere sortes;
hic amor, haec patria est …
desine meque tuis incendere teque querelis;
Italiam non sponte sequor.

Aeneid IV, ll. 333–347; 360–361

. . . At last
he ventured a few words: "I . . . you have done me
so many kindnesses, and you could count them all.
I shall never deny what you deserve, my queen,
never regret my memories of Dido, not while I
can recall myself and draw the breath of life.
I'll state my case in a few words. I never dreamed
I'd keep my flight a secret. Don't imagine that.

Nor did I once extend a bridegroom's torch
or enter into a marriage pact with you.
If the Fates had left me free to live my life,
to arrange my own affairs of my own free will,
Troy is the city, first of all, that I'd safeguard,
Troy and all that's left of my people whom I cherish.
The grand palace of Priam would stand once more,
with my own hands I would fortify a second Troy
to house my Trojans in defeat. But not now.
Grynean Apollo's oracle says that I must seize
on Italy's noble land, his Lycian lots say 'Italy!'
There lies my love, there lies my homeland now ...
... Come, stop inflaming us both
with your appeals. I set sail for Italy –
all against my will."

[Robert Fagles]

Dear oh dear, Aeneas. Terrible dumping technique. Now Dido really does blow up. She's angry for a lot of reasons – one might point out, for instance, that the affair hadn't been entirely one way, but that Aeneas had been having a fabulous time, feasting each night at Dido's table and indeed enjoying her bounty, as it were, in other ways. Largely, however, she is furious because he's shown complete emotional ineptitude and appears to be utterly lacking in empathy. "*Num lumina flexit?*" she asks. "*Num lacrimas victus dedit aut miseratus amantem est?"* – "Has he even looked at me? Has he softened, or lost a tear for someone who loved him?" No, Dido, he bloody well has not.

This is a textbook case. Dido's getting more and more angry because Aeneas is looking less and less like he gave a damn in the first place. The touch of psycho ex-girlfriend behaviour that Dido indulges in here would have been avoidable if Aeneas had been less cold, less unfeeling.

Dido Building Carthage, *by JMW Turner.*
She was a true grafter – till Aeneas came along . . .

The reality is, of course, that Aeneas actually is upset – he's just so crippled by his typical male inarticulacy he can't express it:

At pius Aeneas, quamquam lenire dolentem
solando cupit et dictis auertere curas,
multa gemens magnoque animum labefactus amore
iussa tamen diuum exsequitur classemque reuisit.

Aeneid IV, ll. 393–396

But Aeneas
is driven by duty now. Strongly as he longs
to ease and allay her sorrow, speak to her,
turn away her anguish with reassurance, still,
moaning deeply, heart shattered by his great love,
in spite of all he obeys the gods' commands
and back he goes to his ships

[Robert Fagles]

I'm afraid this is totally useless. And Aeneas is encouraged
in his no-good attitude, I am afraid to say, by another visita-
tion from a male friend, in this case the god Mercury, who
rather annoyingly tells him to buck up on the grounds that
women are always going to be moody and irrational – using
the irritatingly quotable line "*uarium et mutabile semper femina*" – "woman is always a capricious and changeable thing".
Compare – also aggravatingly – the Duke of Mantua's
famous canzone from Verdi's *Rigoletto*: "*La donna è
mobile/Qual piuma al vento,/Muta d'accento – e di pensiero.*"
– "Woman is fickle, like a feather in the wind, she changes

her voice and her thoughts." Dreadfully unfair, of course: Dido has been nothing if not consistent.

One other point. Dido would have been well-advised to learn from Aeneas's relationship history, which, had she taken any notice of it at all when he told her all about it, would have given her a bit of warning about his ineptitude in dealing with the ladies.

The way the early part of the *Aeneid* is constructed is this. Book One tells of the Trojans' arrival in Africa. After a bit of to-ing and fro-ing they are welcomed by the Carthaginians and sit down to dinner. Aeneas is asked to tell the assembled company about his recent travels, and he does: the whole of Books Two and Three are a flashback, with Aeneas relating what happened at the sack of Troy and his crew's subsequent Mediterranean peregrinations.

In Book Two, the part where Aeneas tells the Carthaginians about the end of Troy, we are introduced to Aeneas's ex: his wife Creusa, mother of his child Ascanius (sometimes called Iulus; thus, rather fancifully, supposed to be the founder of Julius Caesar's tribe, the Julii). It becomes clear that Aeneas's treatment of his wife classes him as *particularly* poor boyfriend material.

What happens is this. During the endgame of the siege, when the city, thanks to the Trojan Horse, is overrun by the Greeks, Aeneas receives a pair of supernatural visitations.

These are from the ghost of the Trojan hero Hector (this bit making a particularly fine and rather creepy scene in the first part of Berlioz's *Les Troyens*) and his mother, the goddess Venus (patroness of lovers and love-rats, how terribly appropriate). Aeneas happens to be out and about in the city at the time of these visions, where he witnesses various atrocities, such as the slaughter of the aged King Priam.

Fear Greeks bearing gifts and all that. . . .
The Trojan Horse

The messages of Hector and his mother are clear. Hector says: get the hell out of Troy – your destiny is to transport your people to the site of a great future city (Rome, of course). His mother says: why the hell are you rampaging round the streets when at home you have an incapacitated father, a small son and a wife who are going to cop it sharpish unless you get back there right now to look after them?

Aeneas does do what she says: he goes back home. Unfortunately, there he meets a setback. His father, Anchises, a stubborn old bird, is refusing to leave the family home, and certainly won't countenance the idea of exile. At that, Aeneas completely loses his head, straps on his armour once more and makes to rush off out again to die in battle – "*numquam omnes hodie moriemur inulti*" – "we will not all today die unavenged", he says. Poor Creusa actually has to run to the front door, grab hold of his feet (in Latin, rather wonderfully, "*haerebat*", she "sticks to them") and beg him not to forget his family. What Aeneas is about to do is the worst of all worlds – neither making an escape from Troy in accordance with his destiny, nor making any attempt to defend his son, father and wife.

Creusa makes this rather sad speech:

"*Si periturus abis, et nos rape in omnia tecum;*
sin aliquam expertus sumptis spem ponis in armis,
hanc primum tutare domum. cui paruus Iulus,
cui pater et coniunx quondam tua dicta relinquor?"

Aeneid II, ll. 675–8

"If you are going off to die," she begged,
"then take us with you too,
to face the worst together. But if your battles
teach you to hope in arms, the arms you buckle on,
your first duty should be to guard our house.

Desert us, leave us now – to whom? Whom?
Little Iulus, your father and your wife,
so I once was called."

[Robert Fagles]

Well said, Creusa! Aeneas is behaving like an idiot (not everyone is obliged to agree with me; indeed, I remember making this exact point in 1988 to my splendid Latin teacher Miss Smart, and she was really quite put out that Aeneas could be regarded as less than thoroughly decent).

He doesn't answer her. As becomes even clearer from his dealings with Dido, he's not very good about answering his lady friends at moments of high drama. On this occasion he is, in fact, saved the trouble by yet another supernatural event – a flame seems to play over Ascanius's head, and then a comet shoots through the night sky. Finally the males of the family are convinced it's time to leave. You can almost sense the Olympians wearily wondering how many visions or portents are going to be required before this lot actually gets with the programme.

So, Aeneas picks up his dad and hoists him on to his back. He holds the little Ascanius by the hand. Creusa follows behind. Off they go.

Then something terrible happens. When they arrive at the agreed mustering point, a tomb outside the city, Aeneas realises Creusa is not there. At no point during their escape, he admits, did he *"respexi animumue reflexi"*, "look back or even give her a thought". Dreadful behaviour, and a hint, had Dido chosen to take it, that Aeneas could be both incredibly rash and utterly heedless of those he loves. Aeneas, meanwhile, is of course devastated about the loss of his wife, and runs back into the city to try to find her.

Too. Bloody. Late.

Where's Creusa?
Bernini's statue of Aeneas, Anchises and Ascanius

Back to Book Four. I must concede here that Dido does go a little bit overboard. Yes, she overreacts. I mean, she constructs a funeral pyre, climbs atop it, and runs herself through with Aeneas's own sword (nice bit of phallic imagery there).

Still, had Aeneas been less of a bounder, doubtless Dido wouldn't have gone for the big gesture. And his bad behaviour, it turns out, does him absolutely no good at all.

First of all, he thinks better of his behaviour after her death. (Yet again – too late.) This is what happens. Later on in the poem, in Book Six, he pays a visit to the Underworld, where he meets his father (by now also dead) and has the future of Rome usefully sketched out for him. But he also runs into Dido, who is with the other ghosts "*quos durus amor crudeli tabe peredit*", "whom harsh love has consumed with cruel wasting-away".

At this point, Aeneas is the one who gets weepy:

"inuitus, regina, tuo de litore cessi.
sed me iussa deum, quae nunc has ire per umbras,
per loca senta situ cogunt noctemque profundam,
imperiis egere suis; nec credere quiui
hunc tantum tibi me discessu ferre dolorem.
siste gradum teque aspectu ne subtrahe nostro.
quem fugis? extremum fato quod te adloquor hoc est."
talibus Aeneas ardentem et torua tuentem
lenibat dictis animum lacrimas ciebat.

illa solo fixos oculos auersa tenebat
nec magis incepto uultum sermone mouetur
quam si dura silex aut stet Marpesia cautes.

Aeneid VI, ll. 460–471

I left your shores, my Queen, against my will. Yes,
the will of the gods, that drives me through the shadows now,
these mouldering places so forelorn, this deep unfathomed
                 night –
their decrees have forced me on. Nor did I ever dream
my leaving could have brought you so much grief.
Stay a moment. Don't withdraw from my sight.
Running away – from whom? This is the last word
that Fate allows me to say to you. The last."

Aeneas, with such appeals, with welling tears,
tried to soothe her rage, her wild fiery glance.
But she, her eyes fixed on the ground, turned away,
her features no more moved by his pleas as he talked on
than if she were set in stony flint or Parian marble rock.

[Robert Fagles]

That's the Latin equivalent of: talk to the hand.

In fact, Dido's hatred is so profound that it (supposedly) causes terrible enmity between their respective nations, leading, in real history, to the three Punic Wars between Rome and Carthage, which was, in its time, the major Mediterranean seafaring power.

The conflict rumbled on for a century, and it was quite touch and go at times – these were the wars in which Hannibal crossed the Alps with his elephants, and invaded Italy. The conflict permanently ground to a halt in 149 BC, when Carthage was razed to the ground after a three-year siege. That was after a concerted political campaign in Rome by people like Cato the Elder, who is supposed to have finished all his speeches with the words "*delenda est Carthago*", "Carthage must be destroyed". A useful phrase, when applied to private enemies, to mutter under one's breath even today.

The upshot of this is: it would have been better all round if Aeneas had shown just a touch more consideration in the first place, wouldn't you say?

VI. LOVE HURTS

Miser Catullus, desinas ineptire
et quod uides perisse perditum ducas.
Wretched Catullus, you should stop fooling
And what you know you've lost, admit losing.
Catullus, Poem Eight

L ove's a disease. The ancients knew it full well. Latin and
Greek poetry is full of metaphors relating love to sick-
ness and wounds. ("*uulnus*" is the Latin for wound, as in
"vulnerable", as one tends to be, in love.) It's not for nothing
that Cupid's *modus operandi* involves piercing you in the
heart with an arrow. Love just isn't necessarily very pleasant
all the time.

Even the exciting opening rounds of an affair can bring
disconcerting physiological effects. As Robert Graves says in
his poem "Symptoms of Love": "Love is a universal
migraine,/A bright stain on the vision/Blotting out reason."

Here's Catullus's Poem 51 (actually a translation of a
famous poem by the Greek writer Sappho). It's a fabulous
sketch of desire and jealousy: the narrator is watching, hor-
rified, as a rival chats up his loved one. Ever had that feeling
where your legs seem to vanish and there's a roaring in your
ears? This is it – which Byron, in his translation, rather struggles to convey.

Ille mi par esse deo videtur,
ille, si fas est, superare diuos,
qui sedens aduersus identidem te
spectat et audit

dulce ridentem, misero quod omnis
eripit sensus mihi: nam simul te,
Lesbia, aspexi, nihil est super mi
[uocis in ore]

lingua sed torpet, tenuis sub artus
flamma demanat, sonitu suopte
tintinant aures, gemina teguntur
lumina nocte.

otium, Catulle, tibi molestum est:
otio exsultas nimiumque gestis:
otium et reges prius et beatas
perdidit urbes.

Equal to Jove, that youth must be,
Greater than Jove, he seems to me,
Who, free from Jealousy's alarms,
Securely, views thy matchless charms;
That cheek, which ever dimpling glows,

That mouth, from whence such music flows,
To him, alike, are always known,
Reserv'd for him, and him alone.
Ah! Lesbia! though 'tis death to me,
I cannot choose but look on thee.
But, at the sight, my senses fly,
I needs must gaze, but gazing die;
Whilst trembling with a thousand fears,
Parch'd to the throat, my tongue adheres,
My pulse beats quick, my breath heaves short,
My limbs deny their slight support;
Cold dews my pallid face o'erspread,
With deadly languor droops my head,
My eyes refuse the cheering light,
Their orbs are veil'd in starless night;
Such pangs my nature sinks beneath,
And feels a temporary death.

(For the record that last verse, omitted by Byron, runs in James Michie's translation: "Sloth is your enemy, your disease, Catullus;/You revel in it, crave it, and adore it./By what else were great kings and flourishing cities/Ruined but sloth?")

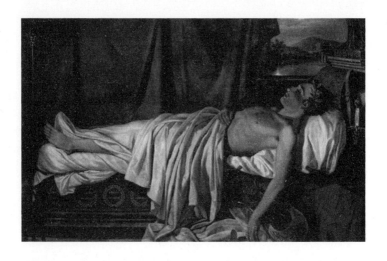

Lord Byron, a true Latin lover, not so much suffering from lovesickness, as actually on his deathbed. By Joseph-Denis Odevaere, c.1826

Catullus is brilliant on the paradoxical nature of love, the anguish of a love-hate relationship. Let's take a closer look at the famous, two-line poem with which this book opened:

Odi et amo. Quare id faciam, fortasse requiris?
nescio, sed fieri sentio, et excrucior.

I hate and love. Why do I do this, perhaps you ask?
I don't know. But I feel it's being done to me, and the
pain is crucifixion.

It's such a tightly constructed poem – just 14 words – and yet it immediately sweeps you into the thick of an utterly vivid emotional world. It captures exactly what's going on when you are painfully in love: the paradox that you are your own worst enemy (you're the one doing the loving, the hating) and, simultaneously, you are a powerless victim of unquenchable feelings (something's being done to you). The hefty, loaded "*excrucior*", which means "I am being tortured", or "I am being crucified", pierces like a dagger in a poem that otherwise uses ordinary, simple language. Suddenly we're reminded of (say) Spartacus's runaway slaves nailed to crosses for 100 miles along the Appian Way. That's love for you, says Catullus: slow, grotesque, ignominious, servile death.

Catullus really drives home the physical and mental pain of heartbreak, though, in his Poem 76:

Siqua recordanti benefacta priora uoluptas
 est homini, cum se cogitat esse pium,
nec sanctam uiolasse fidem, nec foedere ullo
 diuum ad fallendos numine abusum homines,
multa parata manent in longa aetate, Catulle,
 ex hoc ingrato gaudia amore tibi.
nam quaecumque homines bene cuiquam aut dicere possunt
 aut facere, haec a te dictaque factaque sunt.
omnia quae ingratae perierunt credita menti.

quare iam te cur amplius excrucies?
quin tu animo offirmas atque istinc teque reducis
  et dis inuitis desinis esse miser?
difficile est longum subito deponere amorem
  difficile est, uerum hoc est tibi peruincendum.
hoc facias, siue id non pote siue pote.

  O di, si uestrum est misereri aut si quibus umquam
extremam iam ipsa in morte tulistis opem,
  me miserum aspicite et, si uitam puriter egi,
eripite hanc pestem perniciemque mihi,
  quae mihi subrepens imos ut torpor in artus
expulit ex omni pectore laetitias.
  non iam illud quaero, contra me ut diligat illa,
aut, quod non potis est, esse pudica uelit:
  ipse ualere opto et taetrum hunc deponere morbum.
O di, reddite mi hoc pro pietate mea.

If there's some pleasure, looking back, in feeling
Conscious of good deeds done to fellow men,
Duties performed, promises kept, fair dealing
And no abuse of the name of heaven – why, then,
Catullus, in the life that lies ahead
You have a huge store of enjoyment banked;
For what a friend can say or do you said
And did to help her – and were never thanked;
All the good will you lent was lost on her.

Why let the thought torture you any more?
Toughen your will, be what you once were,
Shrug off the misery that the gods abhor.
It's hard to throw aside love of such long
Standing; it's hard, yet somehow must be done.
There lies your only hope. Whether you're strong
Enough or not, the fight has to be won.
Gods, if you deal in pity, if you lean
Over the dying, easing their last breath,
Look on my trouble and, if mine has been
A pure life, rid me of this plague, this death,
Which creeping through my limbs makes me all numb
And drives joy out of me. I've ceased to hope
That she'll return my love, still less become
Faithful, for that's something beyond her scope.
But, gods, if I have served you, grant my prayer:
Health, and an end to this diseased despair.

[James Michie]

Catullus is coming to a hideously painful realisation:
what he desired from Lesbia, she will never be able to give
him. He wanted faithfulness, and he wanted devotion. Since
neither are forthcoming, the brutal truth is that the love
affair needs to end.

But this is grotesquely difficult. On the one hand, he can
see his situation rationally – that is, he perceives that this

pain will pass. He knows, for instance, that his behaviour has been fair and true; he has acted reasonably according to his own moral code. He therefore has a degree of confidence that he will enjoy a happy life, in the end.

But, on the other hand, he finds the present reality almost unendurable: the dread love disease is punishing him hard. He prays to the gods to cure him – about all he can do, poor man. For, as anyone who's had their heart broken knows, only time will make you better. And when you're in the thick of that torment, you feel like you'll never, ever recover. He's at that dreadful rock-bottom moment when you're convinced (despite what your rational mind is telling you) that you'll never smile again, never have sex again, and certainly never be loved again.

At least he has objectified his painful feelings, classified them as an ailment, rather than as some inextricable part of him. This way, there is hope: one can recover from illness (or, admittedly, die, but let's not take an unduly bleak view of the situation). Were this book into affirmations, it might prescribe the daily repetition of the line "*eripite hanc pestem perniciemque mihi*", "rid me of this plague, this death", for those exiting a toxic relationship. As Catullus points out, it is not easy to put aside love. But he must do it if he can, or even if he feels he can't.

Catullus repeats this point to himself over four lines, from the first "*difficile est*", "it's hard", halfway through the poem. He is having to force himself to be strong: that, I am afraid, is the way it goes.

Another great poem of mingled determination and desolation is Catullus's Poem Eight – I think this is up there among the greatest poems of antiquity:

Miser Catulle, desinas ineptire
et quod uides perisse perditum ducas.
fulsere quondam candidi tibi soles,
cum uentitabas quo puella ducebat
amata nobis quantum amabitur nulla.
ibi illa multa cum iocosa fiebant
quae tu uolebas nec puella nolebat,
fulsere uere candidi tibi soles.
nunc iam illa non uolt, tu quoque, impotens, noli,
nec quae fugit sectare nec miser uiue,
sed obstinata mente perfer, obdura.
uale, puella. iam Catullus obdurat
nec te requiret nec rogabit inuitam.
at tu dolebis cum rogaberis nulla.
scelesta, uae te, quae tibi manet uita?
quis nunc te adibit? cui uideberis bella?
quem nunc amabis? cuius esse diceris?
quem basiabis? cui labella mordebis?
at tu, Catulle, destinatus obdura.

Enough, Catullus, of this silly whining;
What you can see is lost, write off as lost.
Not long ago the sun was always shining,
And, loved as no girl ever will be loved,
She led the way and you went dancing after.
Those were the days of lovers' games and laughter
When anything you wanted she approved;
That was a time when the sun really shone.
But now she's cold, you too must learn to cool;
Weak though you are, stop groping for what's gone,
Stop whimpering, and be stoically resigned.
Goodbye my girl. Catullus from now on
Is adamant: he has made up his mind:
He won't beg for your favour like a bone.
You'll feel the cold, though, you damned bitch,
                          when men
Leave you alone. What life will you have then?
Who'll visit you? Who'll think you beautiful? Who'll
Be loved by you? Parade you as his own?
Whom will you kiss and nibble then?
                      Oh fool,
Catullus, stop this, stand firm, become stone.

                          [James Michie]

There's a nice Scots translation of this by Douglas Young
that renders the last few lines:

... What lad'll come ye near?
Wha'll think ye bonnie? Wha'll ye cuddle nou?
Whas lass be caad? Wha kiss? Or pree whas mou?
Och, c'wa, Catullus, stievlie nou. Be sweir.

Catullus is, as it were, addressing himself inside his head, as in Poem 76. He's veering between a grim resolve to draw a line under his old affair and a certain wistfulness. Somewhere, deep in his bones, he wishes he and Lesbia were still together.

It's quite a different sort of love affair – this one ends because of the traumas of guilt rather than those of rejection – but here's Laura Jesson in *Brief Encounter*, trying to convince herself to be strong, and failing – very Catullan:

"This can't last. This misery can't last. I must remember that and t ry to control myself. Nothing lasts really. Neither happiness nor despair. Not even life lasts ve ry long. There'll come a time in the future when I shan't mind about this any more, when I can look back and say quite peacefully and cheerfully how silly I was. No, no, I don't want that time to come ever. I want to remember eve ry minute, always, always to the end of my days."

"*Uale, puella. iam Catullus obdurat/nec te requiret nec rogabit inuitam*" – "Goodbye my girl. Catullus from now

Laura Jesson in Brief Encounter *expresses
a very Catullan sensibility*

on/Is adamant: he has made up his mind:/He won't beg for your favour like a bone."

In other words: you will not text the ex, you will not phone the ex, you will remove the number from your handset, on no account will you drink and dial. Move swiftly and safely away from the telephone and secure the area.

When Catullus goes on to ask those rhetorical questions towards the end of the poem (*"cui uideberis bella?"* – "who'll think you beautiful?", and so on) at least two things are going on. First, he really suspects that far from being lonely,

Lesbia's going to have men queuing round the block for her, particularly given the record for a roving eye he's accorded her in other poems. Second, he's remembering the times that he did all those pleasant things, kissing her and touching her and telling her she was gorgeous.

My friend Josh points out a further layer. The person whom Catullus is ostensibly addressing is Lesbia, but at some point this slips, and he addresses himself. Inwardly he's thinking, "It's me who's never going to be kissed again – not by her, not by anyone." It's the dread end-of-relationship feeling, when you believe yourself utterly unlovable and are convinced you're love life is over for ever.

All of that is why he has to pull himself up so suddenly in the last line – "*destinatus obdura*", "stop this, stand firm, become stone", he tells himself. If you are into affirmations, that would be another one to chant into the mirror each morning. Go on: I dare you. Do the Scots version if you fancy.

VII. CURES FOR LOVE

There ain't no cure for love.
   There ain't no cure for love.
All the rocket ships are climbing through the sky,
The holy books are open wide,
The doctors working day and night,
But they'll never ever find that cure,
The cure for love.

So claims the philosopher and sage Leonard Cohen.

Ovid, however, would beg to differ. Apart from writing his *Ars Amatoria* about how to find and keep a lover, he also produced a work called the *Remedia Amoris* (*Cures for Love*) on how to get out of a relationship – and get over it. Nor is he one for false modesty. If Dido had been able to read his poem, he claims, she wouldn't have come a cropper like she did.

His first piece of advice is this: if you want to exit a love affair with your heart intact, do so sooner rather than later.

If you're planning to uproot a tree, he points out, it's easy to do when it's a seedling, but not so easy when it's a great branching thing. He gives the example of Myrrha, one of the most pervy stories of Greek legend. "*Si cito sensisses quantum peccare parares,/non tegeres uultus cortice, Myrrha, tuos*" – "Had you, Myrrha, realised sooner what a dreadful crime you were planning, your face would not be covered with bark today." The rather gruesome story is this: Myrrha developed an overwhelming passion for her own father. She tricked him into sleeping with her. When he discovered the identity of his mysterious night visitor (by the simple act of switching on the bedroom light), he tried to kill her. But the gods turned her into a myrrh tree, and later, still as a tree, she gave birth to the gorgeous Adonis. It's a story beautifully told in Ovid's *Metamorphoses*.

The poet Lucretius was also extremely keen on the notion of knocking love on the head sharpish. He was writing rather earlier than Ovid – he was born in about 94 BC and died around 49 BC, about six years before Ovid was born. His only work is the hefty *De Rerum Natura*, *On the Nature of Things* (often known as *On the Nature of the Universe*), a great didactic poem in big crunchy hexameters.

Suffused with the teachings of Epicurean philosophy, its subject is how the universe works: atomic theory, theories of perception, how civilisation came about … laced with his savagely sceptical attitude towards superstition and religion.

Contrary to popular belief, Epicureanism was not particularly about having a glamorously sybaritic lifestyle, being waited on by naked slaves and eating endless good dinners, but really about "*ataraxia*", a Greek word meaning freedom from turmoil. For the Epicurean, pleasure was important, but it had to be manageable. The kind of hectic, unreliable pleasure we get from romantic love, which can all too easily turn into pain and misery, was out. Epicureans, therefore, proposed a pretty detached attitude to love. Sex, according to them, was OK; getting emotionally embroiled was absolutely not. It only leads to trouble.

> *nam uitare, plagas in amoris ne iaciamur,*
> *non ita difficile est quam captum retibus ipsis*
> *exire et ualidos ueneris perrumpere nodos.*
>
> *De Rerum Natura* IV, ll. 1146–1148

Take my advice and keep your fancy free.
For to avoid being captured in the snares of love
Is not so difficult as to escape
Once in, and break the powerful knots of Venus.

[Ronald Melville]

Lucretius goes on to suggest that one focus on the faults of the ex-girlfriend or boyfriend: go on, make a list! A friend of mine once told me in deep seriousness that a great way to stop fancying someone unsuitable is to identify a single physical characteristic that you're not crazy about (there's always a little pot belly or a thin wrist or a hairy hand) and think about it really, really hard. Ross does this in relation to Rachel in an episode of *Friends*, though it's a bit of a struggle for him because, really, he's pretty into her. He manages to come up with "a little spoiled", "a little ditzy", and "her ankles are a little chubby". I think Lucretius would expect better.

Epicurus of Samos (341–270 BC), founder of the Epicurean school – his philosophy was sadly not all about five-course lunches at Le Bernardin . . .

Very practical advice is to throw yourself into work, jolly efficacious in my experience. If you give yourself time to mope about your heartbreak, then mope you will. In Latin, throwing yourself into work means swapping "*otium*", "leisure", for businesslike getting-on-with-things, "*negotium*". Like Catullus says in his Poem 51, *otium* can be a very destructive force: "*otium et reges prius et beatas/perdidit urbes*" – "leisure in the past has destroyed rulers and prosperous cities." Here's Ovid again:

desidiam puer ille sequi solet, odit agentes:
  da uacuae menti, quo teneatur, opus.
sunt fora, sunt leges, sunt, quos tuearis, amici:
  uade per urbanae splendida castra togae.
uel tu sanguinei iuuenalia munera Martis
  suspice: deliciae iam tibi terga dabunt.
ecce, fugax Parthus, magni noua causa triumphi,
  iam uidet in campis Caesaris arma suis:
uince Cupidineas pariter Parthasque sagittas,
  et refer ad patrios bina tropaea deos.
ut semel Aetola Venus est a cuspide laesa,
  mandat amatori bella gerenda suo.
quaeritis, Aegisthus quare sit factus adulter?
  in promptu causa est: desidiosus erat.

Remedia Amoris, ll. 148–162

Cupid homes in on sloth, detests the active – so give that
    Bored mind of yours some really absorbing work:
Public business, the law-courts, a friend in need of
                         Counsel–
    Join the smart urban-legal civilian set!
Or else be a soldier (the young man's proper profession),
    And watch your erotic frolics quit the field!
The fugitive Parthian, fresh cause of a glorious triumph,
    Sees Caesar's troops come crunching across his steppes;
So conquer Love's *and* the Parthians' arrows together,
    Score a double, bring home to your country's gods
Not one but two trophies. When pricked by Diomedes'
                        weapon
    Venus quit fighting, left her lover Mars
To bear the brunt of the battle. Why do you think
                        Aegisthus
    Became an adulterer? Easy: he was idle – and bored.

                                  [Peter Green]

    The Parthians were Rome's arch-enemies – difficult-to-defeat warriors from what's now Iran who controlled an empire covering a vast swathe of the Middle East. Aegisthus was the thoroughly nasty piece of work who took up with Clytemnestra while her husband, Agamemnon, was off for ten years at the Trojan War. Agamemnon was killed by the lovers when he returned to Greece, the subject of the first play in Aeschylus's far-from-cheerful dramatic trilogy, the *Oresteia*. It's a typical piece of Ovidian tomfoolery to suggest that Aegisthus, the weighty Aeschylean character, was really a proto-Latin lover, a bored *flâneur*. Diomedes, meanwhile, was a Greek hero, whose arrow wounded Venus when she took part in the fighting at Troy (so Ovid's joke is that he quite literally defeated Love in battle).

If you can, give yourself a complete change of scene:

> *tu tantum, quamuis firmis retinebere uinclis,*
> *i procul, et longas carpere perge uias.*
> *flebis, et occurret desertae nomen amicae,*
> *stabit et in media pes tibi saepe uia.*
> *sed quanto minus ire uoles, magis ire memento,*
> *perfer, et inuitos currere coge pedes.*
>
> *Remedia Amoris*, ll. 213–218

Though the chains that hold you are strong, you just
                  need to make a lengthy
Journey, go far away: you'll weep, your mind
Will dwell on the name of your deserted mistress,
    Your foot often hesitate midway
Through your travels. The less you're anxious to go,
               the more you
    Should make sure of going, persist,
Force yourself to hurry regardless.   [Peter Green]

It's a time-honoured trick, that: get the hell out. Jane Eyre does it when her wedding to Rochester is unavoidably prevented; Alec Harvey does it in *Brief Encounter* (sob).

Propertius takes exactly the same view when he wants to forget about his ex-girlfriend, Cynthia. A holiday in Greece is what he had in mind: you could do worse.

> *magnum iter ad doctas proficisci cogor Athenas*
> *ut me longa graui soluat amore uia.*
> *... unum erit auxilium: mutatis Cynthia terris*
> *quantum oculis, animo tam procul ibit amor.*

III. 21, ll. 1–2, 8–10

I must away on the great journey to learned Athens
To rid myself by travel of love's burden.
... The only cure will be foreign travel. Then love
Will go as far from mind as Cynthia from sight.

[Guy Lee]

Athens offered all manner of opportunities for improving activities: it was *the* place to go if you wanted to study philosophy. So Propertius has lined up some time with the followers of Plato and Epicurus – the latter, as we've seen, could probably offer him all sorts of advice on his love problem. He's hoping that "*aut spatia annorum aut longa interualla profundi/lenibunt tacito uulnera nostra sinu*" – "Either the

119

lapse of years or the deep's long distances/Will heal the wound in my silent breast".

Don't spend great tracts of time on your own. Solitude is the worst thing for a broken heart: too much brooding. You don't want to end up like Miss Havisham, do you? Good: so make sure you line up lots of social events and evenings out with friends. It'll take your mind off everything. *"Tristis eris, si solus eris, dominaeque relictae/ante oculos facies stabit, ut ipsa, tuos"* – "if you're on your own you'll be sad, you'll see your forsaken girl's face in your mind's eye." Lucretius, ever the cynic, counsels a bit of honest-to-goodness casual sex to keep you distracted:

Follow Propertius's advice and take yourself off
to learned (and sunny) Athens to get over your troubles . . .

nam si abest quod ames, praesto simulacra tamen sunt
illius et nomen dulce obuersatur ad auris.
sed fugitare decet simulacra et pabula amoris
absterrere sibi atque alio conuertere mentem
et iacere umorem conlectum in corpora quaeque,
nec retinere, semel conuersum unius amore,
et seruare sibi curam certumque dolorem.

De Rerum Natura IV, ll. 1061–1067

For if what you love is absent, none the less
Its images are there, and the sweet name
Sounds in your ears. Ah, cursed images!
Flee them you must and all the food of love
Reject, and turn the mind away, and throw
The pent-up fluid into other bodies,
And let it go, not with one single love
Straitjacketed, not storing in your heart
The certainty of endless cares and pain.

[Ronald Melville]

Finally, you really do have to stop reading love poetry. It always makes people moony in the end. Remember Captain Benwick in Jane Austen's *Persuasion*? The gloomy one who's lost his fiancée, and who ends up marrying Louisa Musgrove? He's always reciting, with "tremulous feeling, the various lines which imaged a broken heart, or a mind destroyed by wretchedness", moving Anne Elliot to remark that "she thought it was the misfortune of poetry, to be seldom safely enjoyed by those who enjoyed it competely; and that the strong feelings which alone could estimate it truly, were the very feelings which ought to taste it but sparingly".

So, as Ovid says:

eloquar inuitus: teneros ne tange poetas;
    summoueo dotes ipsius ipse meas.
Callimachum fugito, non est inimicus amori;
    et cum Callimacho tu quoque, Coe, noces.
me certe Sappho meliorem fecit amicae,
    nec rigidos mores Teia Musa dedit.
carmina quis potuit tuto legisse Tibulli
    uel tua, cuius opus Cynthia sola fuit?
quis poterit lecto durus discedere Gallo?
    et mea nescioquid carmina tale sonant.

                     Remedia Amoris, ll. 757–766

            What's more, though I hate to say this,
      Love poems are *out*: the ban extends to my own
Collected works. Don't read Callimachus, he's no
                        stranger
    To passion; Philetas too can do you harm.
Sappho, I know, once helped me to soften up my
                        mistress,

And whatever Anacreon offers, it's certainly not
A strict code of morals. But then, who could leaf
                              through Tibullus
    Unscathed, or Propertius, whose single theme was
                              his love
For Cynthia? Who can read Gallus, and end in mere
                              indifference?
    My poems, too, catch something of this mood.

                              [Peter Green]

This is a roll call of the great Greek and Latin love poets, and they are all, including Ovid's own work, now on our banned list.

Luckily there's only one chapter left – you can make an exception for that. It's about Catullus, whom Ovid conveniently leaves out of this list. And it does have a happy ending...

Jane Austen saw that love poetry
was not always the solution for a broken heart ...

VIII. NEXT!

Nulla viri speret sermones esse fideles
No woman should put her faith in what men swear
Catullus, Poem 64

It wasn't just poor old Dido who got given the heave-ho rather precipitously by her rubbish lover (see chapter V, Dumped). There are unforgivable chuckings a-plenty in Latin literature. One of the best, or I should say worst, is by Catullus. It is in Poem 64, his longest, most ambitious and grandest work – an epyllion, or mini-epic. It's a masterpiece.

Ostensibly, the subject of Catullus 64 is the wedding of Peleus and Thetis. In Greek mythology, Peleus was one of the Argonauts, who sailed with Jason to track down the Golden Fleece at Colchis on the Black Sea in modern Georgia. Thetis was a sea goddess – and it was exceptional for a goddess to marry a mortal man, even though Zeus made a habit of bedding mortal women in all sorts of slightly pervy ways – disguised as a swan, a bull and even as a shower of gold. Anyway, as Peleus and chums were sailing towards Colchis, he caught sight of her and a number of other sea nymphs in the water. Catullus rather sexily describes what he got an eyeful of – breasts "*exstantes e gurgite cano*", "standing out from the foamy waves".

It's love at first sight, and the poem switches straight to the wedding, in Thessaly. Catullus describes the incredible splendour of the royal palace:

Candet ebur soliis, collucent pocula mensae,
tota domus gaudet regali splendida gaza

ll. 45–46

Ivory glitters on thrones; on tables, in long lines,
Cups catch the light in unison; the whole house
Smiles with magnificent, royal opulence."

[James Michie]

It's all very Posh and Becks.

Peleus and Thetis, by the way, end up as the parents of the great hero Achilles. Thetis (the lovely Julie Christie in the film *Troy*) is the one who sorts him out with his splendid armour, handmade by the god Hephaestus. She also makes him invincible by dunking him into the River Styx, but carelessly omits his heel (by which she was holding him), hence the phrase Achilles heel, meaning vulnerable spot. But I digress – which is exactly what the poem does.

Just when we think we're about to be told about the food, what the bride was wearing and who was there, with all the lavish detailing of an *OK!* magazine spread, the poem veers off on to something quite different. It starts to describe the coverlet on the couple's bed, on which is embroidered an image of the ancient Greek heroine Ariadne. What happens now is that Ariadne completely takes over the poem. We forget (until those moments when Catullus somewhat pointedly reminds us) that we are supposedly just looking at a wonderful textile. The picture of her takes on a life of its own – just as, sometimes, a really good work of art can suck you in and make you forget that there's a world outside its frame.

It's just the sort of effect Catullus and his peers, the so-called neoteric poets, were interested in – playing around with formal expectations; homing in on arcane detailing; wilfully distorting conventional proportionality... it reminds me a bit (though it's even more extreme) of Thomas Pynchon's novel *The Crying of Lot 49*, in which a hilariously and almost painfully detailed plot precis of an apocryphal Jacobean revenge play called *The Courier's Tragedy*, directed by one Randolph Driblette, occupies an entire seven pages of a slender, 120-page book, ending with: "The fifth act, entirely an anticlimax, is taken up by the bloodbath Gennaro visits on the court of Squamuglia. Every mode of violent death available to Renaissance man, including a lye pit, land mines, a trained falcon with envenom'd talons, is employed." Marvellous stuff. But I digress, again.

So: Ariadne. She was the daughter of King Minos of

Crete – such a powerful ruler that each year the king of Athens, miles away on the Greek mainland, had to send seven girls and seven boys as tribute (that's a euphemism for a fourteen-course dinner) to the Minotaur. That was the hideous half-bull, half-man that Minos had hidden away in the centre of his labyrinthine palace. The Minotaur was, in fact, Minos's stepson; it was the child of his wife Pasiphaë. In one of the more outlandish episodes of classical mythology, Pasiphaë fell in love with a magnificent bull. She got Daedalus (the one who later had that unpleasant episode with his son Icarus and the molten wax) to find a way for her to copulate with the creature. He built her a kind of cow-

The Wedding of Peleus and Thetis, by Cornelisz van Haarlem (1593)
An OK!*-style party by all accounts . . .*

shaped framework, into which she clambered. The bull did its business and, in due course, along came baby Minotaur. Not a particularly attractive infant, I imagine.

One year, the tribute of young men from the king of Athens included the handsome Theseus, his son. Ariadne, Minos's daughter, was so struck with Theseus's dashing good looks that she helped him find a way to kill the Minotaur, her own half-brother. She also famously kitted him out with a ball of string so that he could find his way out of the labyrinth. She put herself out, it is fair to say. Went well beyond the call of mere politeness.

Everything looked good. The Minotaur was killed, Theseus emerged unscathed from the labyrinth, and the pair set sail for Athens. Theseus seemed to be totally into Ariadne, and she was just happily planning herself a fairytale wedding when, on the boat back to Athens, they put in on the island of Naxos for a night of passion. The next morning when she woke up, the ship was just a speck on the horizon. In other words, he'd left her behind on an uninhabited shore after she'd helped him kill her brother. The ungrateful bastard.

That's where the Catullus poem comes in. Here she is (in the embroidery) having a pretty terrible morning watching her fiancé's ship disappear into the distance:

Crete, home of the mistreated Ariadne . . .

haec uestis priscis hominum uariata figuris
heroum mira virtutes indicat arte.
namque fluentisono prospectans litore Diae,
Thesea cedentem celeri cum classe tuetur
indomitos in corde gerens Ariadna furores,
necdum etiam sese quae uisit uisere credit,
utpote fallaci quae tum primum excita somno
desertam in sola miseram se cernat harena.
immemor at iuuenis fugiens pellit uada remis,
irrita uentosae linquens promissa procellae.
quem procul ex alga maestis Minois ocellis,
saxea ut effigies bacchantis, prospicit, eheu,
non flauo retinens subtilem uertice mitram,
non contecta leui uelatum pectus amictu,

non tereti strophio lactentis uincta papillas,
omnia quae toto delapsa e corpore passim
ipsius ante pedes fluctus salis alludebant.

ll. 50–67

Embroidered on this coverlet were figures
Of antique times marvellously representing
Heroic enterprise. Here Ariadne
On the surf-booming shore of Naxos gazes
At Theseus and his shipmates making off
And, still incredulous of what she sees,
Feels love, a wild beast, tear at her: no wonder,
For, having woken from deluding sleep,
She finds herself abandoned pitiably
On the bare sands, while he, oblivious,
Batters the sea with oars, leaving behind
Meaningless promises for the gale to play with.
There on the seaweed fringe the weeping princess
Stares seaward like a maenad carved in stone,
While her heart heaves and swells across the distance.
Gone from her yellow hair the fine-woven bonnet,
Thrown off the light blouse and the delicate scarf
That bound her milk-white breasts – her garments fallen
Loose at her feet and lapped by the salt tide.

[James Michie]

Dear old Catullus can't resist Ariadne's having all her clothes fall off here, quite unnecessarily. But we'll let that pass. The point is that she has committed a range of classic mistakes. She has sold herself short; allowed herself to be used like a complete doormat; and put a terrific amount of trust in someone who hasn't actually earned it.

And so she says:

"Sicine me patriis auectam, perfide, ab aris,
perfide, deserto liquisti in litore, Theseu?
sicine discedens, neglecto numine diuum,
immemor a! deuota domum periuria portas?
nullane res potuit crudelis flectere mentis
consilium? tibi nulla fuit clementia praesto,
immite ut nostri uellet miserescere pectus?
at non haec quondam blanda promissa dedisti
uoce mihi, non haec miserae sperare iubebas,
sed conubia laeta, sed optatos hymenaeos,
quae cuncta aerii discerpunt irrita uenti.
nunc iam nulla uiro iuranti femina credat,
nulla uiri speret sermones esse fideles
quis dum aliquid cupiens animus praegestit apisci
nil metuunt iurare, nihil promittere parcunt,
sed simul ac cupidae mentis satiata libido est,
dicta nihil meminere, nihil periuria curant.

ll. 132–148

"So you were false, so you betrayed me, Theseus!
Did you not lure me from my family altars,
Leave me on this bare shore and sail off, slighting
Not only me but the gods? Ah, you take home
A freight of broken promises and my curse!
Could nothing soften your relentless purpose?
Did mercy never prompt you? Did no scruple
Of pity for me stir in that hard heart?
Soft was the voice with which you once swore love
And gave me expectations, not of this
Nightmare but of the dream I most desired,
The privilege and the happiness of marriage –
Mere waste words now, which the wind tears to shreds.
From now on let no woman put her trust
In a man's vows or a man's wheedling speeches,
For when the lustful mood grips them they're bold
With promises, generous with guarantees;
But once their itch is satisfied they shrug off
Words, they don't mind dishonesty.

[James Michie]

Yes, Ariadne has been treated pretty outrageously. Theseus has had his wicked way and buggered off, the oldest story in the book. She's allowed herself to become completely blinded by love to the extent that she's given over her entire being to a man – a man who turns out to be a cad and a bounder. Not a good idea: she has failed in the important duty to look after number one, to keep something of herself back, to have a beady eye on self-preservation.

Terry Thomas, who played many a bounder to perfection, would have had no problems with the role of Theseus

She has, poor lamb, also entertained fairly high expectations (that is, marriage), of someone of whom she knows very little. By the way, this is not gender-specific. Even though the lines about men's crapitude are wonderfully quotable – "*nunc iam nulla uiro iuranti femina credat,/nulla uiri speret sermones esse fideles*", "No woman should put her faith in a man's oath/And none expect a man's word to be trustworthy" – I am afraid Catullus wrote another poem, Poem 70, which is equally if not more quotable, and in which he had it quite the other way round:

Nulli se dicit mulier mea nubere malle
quam mihi, non si se Iuppiter ipse petat.
dicit – sed mulier cupido quod dicit amanti
in vento et rapida scribere oportet aqua.

She swears she'd rather marry me
Than anyone – even Jupiter,
Supposing he were courting her.
She swears; but what a girl will swear
To the man who loves her ought to be
Scribbled on water, scrawled on air.

[James Michie]

Sir Philip Sidney's translation of the same poem goes like this:

Unto no body my woman saith she had rather a
                              wife bee
then to my self, not though Jove grew a suter of hers.
These be her woordes, but a womans wordes to a
                              love that is eger
in wyndes or waters stremes do require to be writt.

Lovely lines, those. And worth taking the hint: accept with a pinch of salt and a dash of cynicism rashly spoken promises that seem to be designed either to shut one up (Catullus knows that his girlfriend is simply telling him what he wants to hear) or get one into bed.

Ariadne's story actually ends happily, I am pleased to report. First of all, although this is rather cruel of me, Theseus gets his comeuppance. When he is approaching Athens, his home, he is supposed to hoist white sails to let his father, King Aegeus, know he is safe. What with his being a complete idiot, he forgets to do this. Aegeus, thinking his son has come to a sticky end, throws himself off the top of the Acropolis and dashes himself to death against the rocks. Whoops.

And back on Naxos, something truly amazing happens. Here are the lines, but some notes are due first. Iacchus is another name for Bacchus, the god of wine and general mayhem. Satyrs, Sileni and Thyads are fun-loving companions of the god; *"thyrsi"* are ritual rods, *"orgia"* are sacred objects. *"Euhoë"* was the traditional cry of the god's worshippers. Oh yes, and one of their things was to get into a loved-up, trance-like state and rip animals apart, hence the "gobbets of mangled bullock" it mentions. (These people really knew how to party.) Sorry about the rather obscure stuff, but it's definitely worth persisting, and reading aloud the last four or so lines of this extract, because the alliterative effects are quite amazing – you can practically hear the cymbals and drums.

at parte ex alia florens uolitabat Iacchus
cum thiaso Satyrorum et Nysigenis Silenis,
te quarens, Ariadna, tuoque incensus amore...
quae tum alacres passim lymphata mente furebant
euhoe bacchantes euhoe, capita inflectentes.
harum pars tecta quatiebant cuspide thyrsos,
pars e diuolso iactabant membra iuuenco,
pars sese tortis serpentibus incingebant,
pars obscura cauis celebrabant orgia cistis,
orgia quae frustra cupiunt audire profani.
plangebant aliae proceris tympana palmis
aut tereti tenuis tinnitus aere ciebant.
multis raucisonos efflabant cornua bombos
barbaraque horribili stridebat tibia cantu.

ll. 251–264

Another section of the coverlet
Showed virile Bacchus swaggering with his crew
Of Satyrs and the Indian-born Sileni,
Mad for you, Ariadne, flushed with love...
And all around, the maenads pranced in a frenzy,
Crying the ritual cry, "Euhoe! Euhoe!",
Tossing their heads; some of them brandishing
The sacred vine-wreathed rod, some bandying
Gobbets of mangled bullock, others twining
Their waists with belts of writhing snakes, and others
Reverently bearing, deep in caskets,

Arcane things which the uninitiated
Long, but in vain, to see, while others stretched
Fingertips to tattoo the tambourine,
Struck a shrill clang from the semicircular cymbals,
Blew hullabaloo on mooing horns or made
The oriental pipes twitter and scream.

[James Michie]

Bacchus, bless his heart, has fallen in love with Ariadne from afar, and now turns up with his excitable friends to claim her. To be honest, he sounds so much more fun than dreary old Theseus. And all this goes to show that you may lose in love, but there's always someone even more fabulous round the corner; never give up hope. As a wise friend once said to me on the day of a break-up: next!

Bacchus *by Michelangelo, in the wonderful Bargello in Florence*

Appendix: Sex Tips from the Romans

procul hinc, procul este seueri
Prudes, this book ain't for you.

I. The Romans Did It Better

Ask someone to free-associate about ancient Rome, and it's not long, after dutiful mention of "empire" and "straight roads", that they'll come up with "orgies". In fact we seem to carry around with us two rather distinct caricatures of the Romans. There are those who were stern and serious chaps who made long, important speeches in the senate, built marvellous temples and civilised the barbarians by making them wash in hot water and learn the ablative absolute. And then there are the Romans who feasted till they needed to throw up in the vomitorium, enjoyed watching unspeakably violent acts in the gladiatorial arena, and indulged in a great deal of rather pervy sex. Latin teachers generally seem to prefer that first lot, but those naughty, over-indulgent Romans do have a habit of pitching up uninvited, even in the classroom.

What's true is that the Romans had a quite different attitude to sex and sexual imagery than that bequeathed to us, two millennia later, by the accumulated layers of Judaeo-Christian tradition. And what seems clear is that, although in Rome there was a deep concern with morality on the one hand, and suitability of literary material to context on the other (for instance, you don't get explicit sex scenes in high falutin' epic, but it's gloves off for grubby old satire), there's a frankness about sexual matters in art and poetry that can seem bracing to say the least.

For instance, though the emperor Augustus instituted in 18 BC a raft of moralistic laws called the *leges Juliae*, which encouraged marriage and childbearing and specifically outlawed adultery by women, he wasn't what you'd call a prude. He was supposed, for example, to have written the following little ditty:

quod futuit Glaphyran Antonius, hanc mihi poenam
Fulvia constituit, se quoque uti futuam.
Fulviam ego ut futuam? quid si me Manius oret
pedicem? faciam? non puto, si sapiam.
'aut futue; aut pugnemus' ait. quid quod mihi vita
carior est ipsa mentula? signa canant!

Because Antony fucks Glaphyra, Fulvia decided to punish me by making me fuck her. I fuck Fulvia? What if Manius asked me to bugger him, would I do it? I don't think so, not if I had any sense. 'Fuck me, or let's fight,' she says. But my cock's dearer to me than life itself. Let the fanfares sound!

Fulvia was the formidable first wife of Mark Antony, a political and military intriguer off her own bat – she stirred up a rebellion against Augustus (then Octavian) in 41 BC, in the deadly and unstable period shortly after the assassination of Julius Caesar. Octavian was supposed to have written these verses after defeating her uprising at Perugia, in Umbria. (Archaeologists have found lead sling-shot around the site, scratched with rude messages such as "I seek Octavian's arse".)

There was a whole tradition in certain types of Latin poetry of wildly obscene invective against one's enemies – Catullus produced quite a lot of this sort of thing (but better), alongside all those highly wrought poems of intense emotion about his girlfriend Lesbia. This, Poem 88, is one of the most entertaining – one of several epigrams aimed at one Gellius, who'd apparently messed with his girl.

Quid facit is, Gelli, qui cum matre atque sorore
prurit et abiectis peruigilat tunicis?
quid facit is, patruum qui non sinit esse maritum?
ecquid scis quantum suscipiat sceleris?
suscipit, o Gelli, quantum non ultima Tethys
nec genitor Nympharum abluit Oceanus:
nam nihil est quicquam sceleris, quo prodeat ultra,
non si demisso se ipse uoret capite.

Gellius, would you say it was right
For a man to monkey around all night
With his mother and sister, half undressed?
Or to cuckoo his uncle's marital nest?

How much guilt does he bear? Far more
Than Tethys washing her farthest shore
Or Ocean, daddy of nymphs, can clean.
He couldn't do anything more obscene,
Not even if, head between his legs,
He took a swig of his own foul dregs.

[James Michie]

II. Pass the Fig Leaf

Then there was visual art. The fact is that there was a lot of what
we would regard as explicit material knocking pretty casually
around people's houses. The Villa Farnesina in Rome, thought
to be the home of Julia, Augustus's daughter, in what's now the
lovely Trastevere district, was decorated with the most exquisite
wall paintings on erotic subjects, which still survive.

In Augustus's own house, according to Ovid (in the
Tristia, literally "Sadnesses", the poems he wrote from his
exile on the Black Sea) there were "*parua tabella*", "little pan-
els", illustrating "*concubitus uarios Venerisque figuras*", "various sexual unions and positions". At Pompeii, excavations
have turned up all kinds of explicit murals, not to mention
the extremely commonplace use of the phallus carved into
walls or depicted on mosaics as a good luck sign for thresh-
olds or crossroads.

If you were a Roman with a garden or farm, chances are you'd have a statue of the fertility spirit Priapus in it, complete with a large erect penis. There was a pottery in Arezzo where excellent-quality terracotta vessels decorated with erotic subjects were mass-produced. If, as a Roman, you visited public baths (which you almost certainly did), you might encounter mosaics of what classicists euphemistically call "macrophallic" men, that is, men with oversize, erect penises, perhaps there to ward off bad luck. And just as you do now, you would find that walls in public places could be scrawled with obscene graffiti. "*Me me mentulam linge*", "lick my cock", and "*imanis mentula es*", "you're a big prick", are two examples collected from the down-and-dirty alleyways of Rome. (And, before any smart-arses try them out on their Latin teacher, beware that in both cases the spelling and grammar is just as correct as we might expect to see in the average modern public loo.)

Particularly in the nineteenth century, however, sexually explicit Roman objects and art were deemed unsuitable for general consumption. Fig leaves sprouted as if of their own accord to mask the genitals of ancient statuary. The more explicit finds from Pompeii were placed in a special, restricted section at the Naples Museum called the Cabinet of Obscene Objects, out of bounds to the general public. Similarly – absurd and unscholarly as it may seem – at the British

Museum there was something known as the Museum Se c retum, in which "obscene" material was deposited, regardless of where in the world and what historical period it came from. Weaker vessels – the uneducated, the poor, the young, and especially women – needed protection from this sort of stuff, it was felt.

III. *PAS DEVANT LES ENFANTS*

In literary terms a similar process of censorship obtained. For example, Terence's play *Phormio*, in being edited for school use in Britain in 1887, had a character who was supposed to be a pimp, "*leno*", transformed into a merchant, "*mercator*". However, because poetic metre in Latin depends on the number and length of syllables in each line, this change had large knock-on effects, requiring wholesale rewriting to accommodate it. Nor (and this does make me giggle) was it ever explained why a whole lot of girls were constantly hanging around with the "*mercator*".

In the case of the wonderful Catullus, many of his works have been justly admired as masterpieces for centuries. But he was also a writer who variously referred to brushing one's teeth with urine and buggering people who criticised his poems. An 1836 edition, published in Boston, Massachusetts, and "selected and prepared for the use of schools and colleges by FM Hubbard", had this to say about the wielding of the bowdleriser's pen:

"By far the greater part of the poems of Catullus are given in this edition. In making a selection from them, the editor has been desirous to retain every thing which could exhibit his author in his personal character and poetical powers, or throw light upon the tastes and sentiments of his age, and at the same time to exclude all that might offend by its indelicacy, or corrupt by its licentiousness."

In fact he retained only half of Catullus's poems. The part of the poet's "personal character" that delighted in the scabrous or demonstated his cheerful polysexuality was clearly not required, ditto those "tastes and sentiments of his age" not strictly in harmony with the mores of nineteenth-century Boston.

Shockingly, even the 1961 edition prepared by the scholar Christian James Fordyce – which was used in my school in the 1980s – announced in its preface that "a few poems which do not lend themselves to comment in English have been omitted". This was extraordinarily disingenuous: Fordyce omitted 32 poems out of a complete corpus of 113.

And as recently as 1989, there was a full-on hoo-ha when three poems by Catullus were removed from the British A level syllabus by the University of London Schools Examination Board after complaints about their subject-matter. The worst the poetry got was describing a character as "softer than the floppy, cobweb-covered penis of an old man". Quite rightly, this inglorious affair was described as "petty-minded censorship" in a letter to the *Guardian*. I am strongly reminded of Yeats's poem "The Scholars":

Bald heads forgetful of their sins,
Old, learned, respectable bald heads
Edit and annotate the lines
That young men, tossing on their beds,
Rhymed out in love's despair
To flatter beauty's ignorant ear.

All shuffle there; all cough in ink;
All wear the carpet with their shoes;
All think what other people think;
All know the man their neighbour knows.
Lord, what would they say
Did their Catullus walk that way?

"Lend themselves to comment in English": the other side of the coin has been Latin's use as a veil for subject matter deemed unsuitable for mass consumption. Even when the language was in fairly wide circulation as a school and university subject, it remained largely the preserve of educated, well-off men – and thus had its uses as a sort of "club" language. That English law was occluded in Latinate terminology meant that only a select group could access its intricacies; medical Latin had the advantage that patients could be "protected" from the grim Anglo-Saxon realities of their conditions (compare, for example, the mild-sounding "*tinea cruris*" to its frankly horrifying English equivalent, "crutch rot"). And using Latin (or Greek) was clearly a great way to keep writing on sex out of reach of the non-elect. In *The Decline and Fall of the Roman Empire*, Edward Gibbon sketches the "vices" of the empress Theodora. "But," he writes suggestively, "her murmurs, her pleasures, and her arts, must be veiled in the obscurity of a learned language."

An unfortunate side effect (for the censors) of this kind of thing is that the eye tends to get drawn to sections of a text that modestly drop into Latin, since one suspects, or indeed hopes, that they will be racy. At least one book has taken advantage of this association: in 1881, a seventeenth-century pornographic work called *Académie des Dames* came out in a new edition, in French, but with the especially dirty bits in Latin. In this case, the Latin was meant to be understood – it was grammatically straightforward and even came with a crib.

IV. AMOR THE MERRIER

In popular culture those stern Romans have often ganged up with the naughty Romans, shielding their decadence from too clear a view. I'm too young to have seen the TV adaptation of Robert Graves's *I, Claudius* novels when it was first broadcast on the BBC in 1976. But even watching it now, it seems surprisingly explicit. Early in the series, for instance, Julia, Augustus's daughter, is having a massage alongside Antonia, Claudius's mother. Julia gigglingly informs her that Tiberius, her new husband, has a penchant for anal sex. Given the hoo-ha that broke out when *Sex and the City* aired its episode on the subject nearly 30 years on (admittedly post-AIDS), one must assume that because *I, Claudius* was a respectable historical costume drama, whose source material was largely drawn from the second-century biographer Suetonius, it could get away with this sort of bawdiness. *I, Claudius* unleashed other shockers on to an unsuspecting but entranced British public: John Hurt's Caligula shagging his sister; Messalina, Claudius's wife, winning a stamina competition against a famous prostitute; a Roman matron describing her subjection to "beastly obscenities" by Tiberius before stabbing herself to death at a dinner party she'd thrown.

The much-derided 1983 BBC series *The Cleopatras* had similar advantages. Strict historical veracity apparently dictated that the royal slaves ought to be bare-breasted; natural-ly, therefore, the viewers enjoyed something of an eyeful. "I was fourteen then," recalls my friend Paul, wistfully. "Never had I seen so many boobs."

V. THE JOY OF SEX ... AND SEPTEM

Oh, and we were talking about orgies, weren't we? Well, you've got to remember that a standard Roman way of run-ning down your enemies was to accuse them of all sorts of sexual peccadilloes, so you don't necessarily want to believe all this. But since you want to know, I'll give you a few exam-ples. We'll kick off with Tiberius, as told by Suetonius:

> *Secessu uero Caprensi etiam sellaria excogitauit, sedem arca-narum libidinum, in quam undique conquisiti puellarum et exoletorum greges monstrosique concubitus repertores, quos spin-trias appellabat, triplici serie conexi, in uicem incestarent coram ipso, ut aspectu deficientis libidines excitaret.*
>
> *Lives of the Caesars*, III.43

On retiring to Capri he made himself a private sporting-house, where sexual extravagances were practised for his secret pleasure. Bevies of girls and young men, whom he had collected from all over the Empire as adepts in unnatural practices, and known as *spintriae*, would copulate before him in groups of three, to excite his waning passions.

[Robert Graves]

The playboy island of Capri . . .

Then there was Commodus, played by the divine Joaquin Phoenix in Ridley Scott's film *Gladiator*, who spent most of his time according to Gibbon "dissolved in luxury" (wonderful phrase) with a harem of 300 girls and 300 boys.

Even the great poet Horace, and here was something Miss Smart never told us at school, had his special tastes, according to Suetonius – he liked doing it in front of mirrors:

Ad res Venerias intemperantior traditur; nam speculato cubiculo scorta dicitur habuisse disposita, ut quocumque respexisset ibi ei imago coitus referretur.

Life of Horace

Apparently he was immoderately keen on sex; for it's said that in a mirror-lined room he had girls positioned so whichever way he looked he could see a reflection of the sex-act.

Perhaps Horace had been getting ideas from a sex manual, which (little-known fact) the ancient Greeks invented. Erotodidaxis, as this genre of writing was known, even came with its own mythical founder, identified, in the Byzantine encyclopaedia known as the Suda, "the maid of Helen, the wife of Menelaus. She was the first to describe the ways of lying in bed for intercourse, and wrote *On the Postures for Intercourse.*" Authors of sex guides apparently included one Elephantis, who is name-checked by the poet Martial, and said by Suetonius to have been a particular favourite of the emperor Tiberius:

Cubicula plurifariam disposita tabellis ac sigillis lascivissimarum picturarum et figurarum adornavit librisque Elephantidis instruxit, ne cui in opera edenda exemplar imperatae schemae deesset.

Lives of the Caesars, III.34

A number of small rooms were furnished with the most indecent pictures and statuary obtainable, also certain erotic manuals by Elephantis; the inmates of the establishment would know exactly what was expected of them.

[Robert Graves, slightly tweaked]

In *I, Claudius*, mad Caligula gives the obscene old goat Tiberius a copy of Elephantis's book as a present, and asks to borrow it, "when you've finished with it, of course".

Philaenis was another famous author of Greek sex manuals. She was perhaps writing in the fourth or fifth century BC – if she was a woman, that is (since there's a school of thought that suggests these books were actually by men). In 1972 a tiny fragment of her book pitched up – it's amazing what emerges from the sand in Egypt – which said not a great deal more than this: "concerning seductions. So then the seducer must go unadorned and uncombed so that he does not [appear] to the woman to be on the job ... woman is like a goddess ... the ugly one is charming, the older one is like a young girl ..."

Well, that's not going to get you very far, but it seems clear that Ovid, in his *Ars Amatoria*, was influenced by this sort of thing, especially in his section on sexual positions at the end of Book Three. One of the interesting things about this account is that it's not especially about pleasure, it's about how you look when you're at it – sort of Trinny and Susannah applied to sex. (Don't worry, we'll get on to pleasure later.)

ulteriora pudet docuisse, sed alma Dione
    "praecipue nostrum est, quod pudet," inquit "opus."
nota sibi sit quaeque; modos a corpore certos
    sumite: non omnes una figura decet.
quae facie praesignis erit, resupina iaceto;
    spectentur tergo, quis sua terga placent.
Milanion umeris Atalantes crura ferebat:
    si bona sunt, hoc sunt aspicienda modo.
parua uehatur equo: quod erat longissima, numquam
    Thebais Hectoreo nupta resedit equo.
strata premat genibus paulum ceruice reflexa
    femina per longum conspicienda latus.
cui femur est iuuenale, carent quoque pectore menda,
    stet uir, in obliquo fusa sit ipsa toro.
nec tibi turpe puta crinem, ut Phylleia mater,
    soluere, et effusis colla reflecte comis.
tu quoque, cui rugis uterum Lucina notauit,
    ut celer auersis utere Parthus equis.
mille ioci Veneris; simplex minimique laboris,
    cum iacet in dextrum semisupina latus.

                        Ars Amatoria III, ll. 768–788

What's left I blush to tell you; but kindly Venus
    Claims as uniquely hers
All that raises a blush. Each woman should know herself,
    pick methods
    To suit her body: one fashion won't do for all.

Let the girl with the pretty face lie supine, let the lady
    Who boasts a good back be viewed
From behind. Milanion bore Atalanta's legs on
    His shoulders: nice legs should always be used this way.
The petite should ride horse (Andromache, Hector's
    Theban
    Bride, was too tall for these games: no jockey she);
If you're built like a fashion model, with willowy figure,
    Then kneel on the bed, your neck
A little arched; the girl who has perfect legs and bosom
    Should lie sideways on, and make her lover stand.
Don't blush to unbind your hair like some ecstatic maenad
    And tumble long tresses about
Your upcurved throat. If childbirth's seamed your belly
    With wrinkles, then offer a rear
Engagement, Parthian style. Sex has countless positions –
    An easy and undemanding one is to lie
On your right side, half-reclining.   [Peter Green]

If you count this lot up, you've got eight possible positions. Of special note is number three – the girl resting her legs on the bloke's shoulders; let's call it the "Atalanta". She was a mythical heroine who allegedly had fantastic legs, on account of her athleticism. She would marry only the man who could beat her in a running race; the losers were executed as soon as the race was finished. Milanion (often called Hippomenes) did manage to beat her, but only through trickery – he distracted her with three golden apples, which he sneakily threw on to the side of the running track. When she veered off the track and stooped to pick them up, he was able to overtake. It's a story wonderfully told in Ovid's *Metamorphoses*, and translated by Ted Hughes in his *Tales from Ovid*. (It ends badly. Hippomenes and Atalanta had sex in a shrine belonging to Cybele, the mother goddess, who was so angry she turned them both into lions and made them pull her chariot.)

Number four is girl on top: we'll call this the "not-Andromache". It's a good position if you're short, says Ovid, unlike Andromache, who was married to Hector, Troy's greatest hero in the *Iliad*, and was supposedly rather tall. The seventh is a variation on this; let's call it the "Parthian". This involves the woman on top but facing backwards, towards the man's feet, so to speak. It's named "Parthian" after Rome's arch-enemies in the Middle East. Parthia, south-west of the Caspian, controlled huge tracts of the east, including, at its height, modern Iran, Iraq, Armenia, bits of Turkey,

Unlikely inspiration from the Parthians ...

Georgia, Azerbaijan and Afghanistan; even, at one point, parts of Pakistan, Syria, Lebanon, Israel and Palestine. The Parthians were famous for their light brigades of mounted archers, who had a special technique of appearing at speed and then galloping off, shooting steel-tipped arrows from behind, over their shoulders – hence the sexual position. (The Parthians were also a constant thorn in the Romans' side. In 53 BC the millionaire and general Crassus had invaded Parthia with a huge force, but was crushed at the battle of Carrhae. Twenty thousand Roman legionaries were killed and 10,000 taken captive. Crassus's head was taken to the king of Parthia, who at the time was enjoying a performance of Euripides's play *The Bacchae*, which features a decapitation. The lead actor resourcefully grabbed the general's head and used it as a prop.)

Further guidance for the ladies – you have a right to an orgasm, says the utterly commendable Ovid:

sentiat ex imis Venerem resoluta medullis
  femina, et ex aequo res iuuet illa duos.
nec blandae uoces iucundaque murmura cessent
  nec taceant mediis improba uerba iocis.

Ars Amatoria III, l. 793–796

A woman should melt with passion to her very marrow,
  The act should give equal pleasure to them both:

Keep up a flow of seductive whispered endearments,
Use sexy taboo words while you're making love.

[Peter Green]

There's very little in surviving ancient literature on women's sexual pleasure – Ovid is almost unique in being remotely interested in it – though there is the following anecdote, as told by Ovid in his *Metamorphoses* (and also translated by Ted Hughes). Zeus and Hera were arguing about whether men or women derived more pleasure from sex. They decided to check with Tiresias, who, extraordinarily enough, had once been a girl. Tiresias pronounced it was the woman who got the better deal. Wrong answer, as far as Hera was concerned. Furious, she struck him blind – but Jupiter gave him second sight as a compensation. He turns up as a character in dramas by Sophocles and Euripides, and in the *Odyssey*, dispensing more or less sensible insights and prophecies.

Older women are best in bed, according to Ovid:

adde, quod est illis operum prudentia maior,
  solus, et, artifices qui facit, usus adest.
illae munditiis annorum damna rependunt
  et faciunt cura, ne uideantur anus,
utque uelis, Venerem iungunt per mille figuras:
  inuenit plures nulla tabella modos.
illis sentitur non inritata uoluptas;

quod iuuat, ex aequo femina uirque ferant.
odi concubitus, qui non utrumque resoluunt . . .

Ars Amatoria II, ll. 675–783

Besides, they possess a wider range of knowledge
    And experience, the sole source
Of true skill: they make up for their years with
                        sophistication,
    Camouflaging their age through art; they know
A thousand postures – name yours – for making love in,
    More ways than any pillow-book could reveal.
They need no stimuli to warm up their passions –
    Men and women should share the same
Pleasures. I hate it unless both lovers reach a climax . . .

[Peter Green]

Complimenting your partner's performance in bed goes down well. It's always good to have positive feedback, reckons Ovid:

et, quod desierit, uerba querentis habe.
ipsos concubitus, ipsum uenerere licebit,
    quod iuuat, et quaedam gaudia noctis habe.

Art Amatoria II, ll. 306–308

    You can even praise
Her performance in bed, her talent for love-making –
    Spell out what turned you on.   [Peter Green]

We'll end, though, with one of the sexiest poems in Latin literature, the fifth poem of Ovid's first book of *Amores*, beautifully translated by Christopher Marlowe. Do enjoy the large legge and lustie thigh.

> *Aestus erat, mediamque dies exegerat horam;*
> *adposui medio membra leuanda toro.*
> *pars adaperta fuit, pars altera clausa fenestrae,*
> *quale fere siluae lumen habere solent,*
> *qualia sublucent fugiente crepuscula Phoebo,*
> *aut ubi nox abiit, nec tamen orta dies.*
> *illa uerecundis lux est praebenda puellis,*
> *qua timidus latebras speret habere pudor.*
> *ecce, Corinna uenit, tunica uelata recincta,*
> *candida diuidua colla tegente coma -*
> *qualiter in thalamos famosa Semiramis isse*
> *dicitur, et multis Lais amata uiris.*
> *deripui tunicam - nec multum rara nocebat;*
> *pugnabat tunica sed tamen illa tegi;*
> *quae, cum ita pugnaret, tamquam quae uincere nollet,*
> *uicta est non aegre proditione sua.*
> *ut stetit ante oculos posito uelamine nostros,*
> *in toto nusquam corpore menda fuit.*
> *quos umeros, quales uidi tetigique lacertos!*
> *forma papillarum quam fuit apta premi!*
> *quam castigato planus sub pectore uenter!*
> *quantum et quale latus! quam iuuenale femur!*
> *Singula quid referam? nil non laudabile uidi*
> *et nudam pressi corpus ad usque meum.*
> *Cetera quis nescit? lassi requieuimus ambo.*
> *proueniant medii sic mihi saepe dies.*

In summers heate and mid-time of the day
To rest my limbes upon a bed I lay.
One window shut, the other open stood,
Which gave such light, as twincles in a wood,
Like twilight glimps at setting of the Sunne
Or night being past, and yet not day begunne.
Such light to shamefast maidens must be showne,
Where they may sport, and seeme to be unknowne.
Then came Corinna in a long loose gowne,
Her white neck hid with tresses hanging downe:
Resembling fayre Semiramis going to bed
Or Layis of a thousand lovers spread.
I snacht her gowne: being thin, the harme was small,
Yet strivd she to be covered there withall.
And striving thus as one that would be cast,
Betray'd her selfe, and yeelded at the last.
Starke naked as she stood before mine eye,
Not one wen in her body could I spie.
What armes and shoulders did I touch and see,
How apt her breasts were to be prest by me.
How smooth a belly under her wast saw I?
How large a legge, and what a lustie thigh?
To leave the rest, all pleasde me passing well,
I clingd her faire white body, downe she fell,
Judge you the rest, being tirde she bad me kisse;
Jove send me more such after-noones as this.

The Latin Lover's Quick Quote List

quis fallere possit amantem?
Virgil, *Aeneid* IV, l. 296

Don't think you can pull the wool over my eyes, buddy. (Literally: who can deceive a lover?) Said by Dido to the faithless Aeneas.

omnia uincit amor
Virgil, *Eclogues* X, l. 69

Love conquers all. (For optimists.)

labor omnia uincit
Virgil, *Georgics* I, l. 145

Work conquers all. (For pessimists.)

nulla uiri speret sermones esse fideles
Catullus, Poem 64, l. 144

Men are crap. (Literally: No woman should put her faith in what men swear.) Said by poor old Ariadne as Theseus's ship disappears on the horizon leaving her alone on a desert island.

uarium et mutabile semper femina
Virgil, *Aeneid* IV, ll. 569–70

Women are useless. (Literally: woman is always a capricious and changeable thing.) One of the god Mercury's utterly spurious arguments to try to get Aeneas to leave Dido.

da mi basia mille
Catullus, Poem Five, l. 7

Give us a kiss, love. (Literally: give me a thousand kisses.) From the immortal Catullus poem.

et dis inuitis desinis esse miser
Catullus, Poem 76, l. 12

For heaven's sake get over yourself. (Literally: shrug off the misery that the gods hate.) When heartbroken pals need tough love.

uritur et loquitur
Catullus, Poem 83, l. 6

(Literally: she burns and she speaks.) Catullus claims that he can tell Lesbia fancies him because she's always so rude about him (it's that sexual electricity thing, as between Beatrice and Benedick in *Much Ado About Nothing*). To be muttered under the breath when someone's running you down, but in that suspiciously flirty way.

militat omnis amans
Ovid, *Amores,* 1.9, l. 1

You've got to work at love.
(Literally: every lover is a
soldier.)

cetera quid nescit?
Ovid, *Amores,* 1.5, l. 25

Who doesn't know the rest? This
line comes as Ovid describes the
seduction of his girlfriend.
They're in the bedroom, he's got
her clothes off, and, with this
phrase, he discreetly leaves what
follows to our imagination. This
is one to use when passing over
the really juicy bits as you give
an otherwise blow-by-blow
account of your last date.

abeas, pharetrate Cupido
Ovid, *Amores* 2.5, l. 1

Down with love. (Literally: get
away, sharp-shooting Cupid)

**quod sequitur, fugio; quod fugit,
ipse sequor**
Ovid, *Amores* 2.19, l. 36

Play hard to get. (Literally: I flee
from what follows me, and I
follow what flees.)

**sic ego nec sine te nec tecum
uiuere possum**
Ovid, *Amores* 3.11b, l. 39

I can't live with you, I can't live
without you.

tu mihi sola place
Ovid, *Ars Amatoria* I, l. 42

You're the only one for me.

cunctas posse capi: capies, tu modo tende plagas
Ovid, *Ars Amatoria* I, l. 269

Any girl can be had. You've only got to set your traps. (Not strictly true, but useful for those in need of a confidence boost.)

saepe uenit magno faenore tardus Amor
Propertius, I.7, l. 26

When love comes late his tax is often high. (To be uttered sagely at lovelorn oldies or once confirmed singletons.)

nulla prius uasto labentur flumina ponto,/annus et inuersas duxerit ante uices,/ quam tua sub nostro mutetur pectore cura
Propertius, I.15, ll. 29–31

Rivers will flow backwards, the seasons will come in reverse order, before I stop loving you. (One for the Valentine's card.)

una sat est cuiuis femina multa mala
Propertius, II.25, l. 47

One woman is plenty of ills for any man. (Take it however you fancy.)

pacis Amor deus est, pacem ueneramur amantes
Propertius, III.5, l. 1

Make love not war. (Literally: Love is the god of peace; we lovers venerate peace.)

odi profanum uulgus et arceo
Horace, *Odes* 3.1 l. 1

You can't be too picky. (Literally: I hate the profane crowd and avoid it.) From a poem that has admittedly nothing to do with love at all. Still, *odi profanum uulgus* is a marvellous phrase that can be employed in all manner of circumstances, including in the supermarket queue, Fifth Avenue, etc., etc.

I. You are a handsome hero named Perseus. You have boasted to your adoptive father that you can give him the head of the Gorgon Medusa, who can turn a man to stone with a single glance. You manage to kill the Gorgon, and, en route home, you pass a beautiful woman chained to a rock, about to be sacrificed to a ravening sea-monster. Do you:

a) Finish off the monster, claim the girl, and turn her parents into stone using the Gorgon's head when they fail to give you permission to marry her?

b) Finish off the monster, claim the girl, then head for home when her parents are a bit iffy about your marrying her?

c) Sod the girl and the monster, you've got to hurry home immediately; after all you have a Gorgon's head in need of urgent delivery?

II. You are Clytemnestra, queen of Mycenae. Your husband goes off to fight in the Trojan War, having sacrificed your daughter to ensure a fair wind. Do you:

a) Take up with an evil lover, name of Aegisthus, and, when your husband returns from his campaigning, deliberately entangle him in his bath towel so Aegisthus can dispatch him with an axe, thus ensuring the continuing curse of the House of Atreides and a bloodlust that will be sated only when your son is tried and acquitted of your murder?

b) Take up with an evil lover, name of Aegisthus, whom, in the interests of family harmony, you dump when your husband returns from the war?

c) Seek a course of anger-management counselling from a local priest, before instituting divorce proceedings?

III. You are Myrrha, a beautiful princess. You develop unquenchable sexual longing for your father, Cinyras. Do you:

a) Wait until your mother is off celebrating a religious festival, then inveigle yourself into your father's bed night after night under cover of darkness, before being transformed into a myrrh tree by the gods and giving birth to the beautiful Adonis, offspring of your incestuous coupling?

b) Get over it, and marry one of the handsome suitors your parents have lined up for you?

c) Openly and honestly decide to work through your Electra complex with the help of a therapist?

IV. You are a fantastically handsome young swain, son of a river god and a nymph. You pass a prettyish little pond in the woods. Do you:

a) Gaze deeply into its waters, becoming so obsessed with the beautiful creature you see there that you cannot drag yourself away, in time starving to death?

b) Gaze deeply into its waters, but as the lovely creature within is clearly unobtainable, make out with that nymph

Echo (cute but not so great at initiating conversation) who has been coming on to you lately?
c) Gaze deeply into its waters, but realise you are suffering from an extreme form of narcissistic personality disorder, and seek help accordingly?

V. You are Medea, queen of Corinth. Years ago, with your magic powers, you helped your husband, Jason, win the Golden Fleece from your father. But now your husband is preparing to dump you for a younger woman, Glauce. Do you:

a) Pretend to be happy for your rival and present her with a lovely wedding gown and a tiara, which you have in fact smeared with deadly poison; then butcher your young children, since that is clearly the most effective way to spite their father?
b) Shred all Jason's tunics before grabbing the children and taking them back to your family's place in Colchis?
c) Retain a veneer of calm dignity while privately determining to screw Jason in the divorce courts?

Mostly As: Congratulations. You are a heroic lover worthy of legendary status. There is no evil, perversion, violence or impiety to which you would not stoop.

Mostly Bs: You're getting there. Don't give up: you exhibit a promising degree of lust. But you need to ratchet up your depravity. Work on giving in to your most obscene instincts.

Mostly Cs: Forget it. Self-knowledge has no place in the world of legendary lovers. You're not even willing to commit murder in pursuit of your insatiable sexual desires! Drop down to remedial level.

Ten Latin Love Paintings in the National Gallery, London

Titian: *Bacchus and Ariadne.* One of the most wonderful paintings in the gallery, and very Catullus Poem 64. Bacchus is in the very act of leaping out of his chariot to launch himself at the pleasantly surprised Ariadne; she has just been abandoned on the beach at Naxos by Theseus, whose ship can be seen diasppearing into the distance. The gods' companions are playing cymbals and tambourines, dancing wildly, wreathed with snakes. The sky is more blue than you can imagine.

Bacchus and Ariadne, *Titian*

Sebastiano Ricci: *Bacchus and Ariadne*. A different take on the episode. Bacchus and Co. have turned up on Naxos, and Ariadne is still fast asleep and very immodestly naked, flopped on a pile of pink cushions. The god is taking a good long look at her; he's all long-haired androgyny and flower-power.

Bacchus and Ariadne, *Sebastiano Ricci*

Rubens: *Aurora Abducting Cephalus*. Aurora, the goddess of the dawn, fell in love with Cephalus, a huntsman – it's a story told in Ovid's *Metamorphoses*, Book Seven. In this oil sketch, in a beautiful golden haze, she's just stepped down from her chariot and is trying to carry him away with her; his hunting dogs are still dozing in the foreground. But Cephalus loved his wife Procis, and turned the goddess down.

Aurora Abducting Cephalus, *Rubens*

Piero di Cosimo: *A Satyr Mourning over a Nymph*. Despite Cephalus's constancy, the story ended badly. Procis was suspicious of her husband and hid in the woods to keep watch on him. Cephalus mistook her for a wild animal and killed her with his spear. The subject of this strange and compelling painting is probably the dead Procis. A dog mournfully gazes at her and she's cradled by a satyr. In the background is a distant shoreline, with a pelican swimming in the glassy water.

A Satyr Mourning over a Nymph, *Piero di Cosimo*

Botticelli: *Venus and Mars*. It's an allegory, this, of the thought "*omnia uincit amor*" – "love conquers all", a quotation from Virgil's tenth Eclogue. Venus has just (we are supposed to imagine) made love to Mars, god of war. He's fast asleep with his mouth open, and some little satyrs are playing with his helmet and spear: War is disarmed. Venus looks smugly on.

Venus and Mars, *Botticelli*

Pintoricchio: *Penelope with Suitors*. While Odysseus was off in Troy fighting, and then adventuring his way back to Ithaca, he left his wife Penelope at home – for a total of twenty years. During his absence she was badgered by suitors trying to persuade her to do the sensible thing: accept that her husband was dead, and choose a new man. She said she would do so, just as soon as she had finished weaving her father-in-law a shroud (a happy thought for old Laertes, no doubt). Each day she spent busily at the loom; and each night she unpicked the day's work. This hilarious picture shows, cartoon-style, an unperturbed Penelope weaving, as various rakish, codpiece-clad suitors bustle in and attempt to impress her. Odysseus is just coming in through the door on the right, disguised as a beggar. He will shortly kill the suitors with his bow, which hangs on a hook above Penelope's head. In the background, you can also see Odysseus outwitting the sirens, an earlier episode in the poem.

Penelope with Suitors, *Pintoricchio*

Antonio del Pollaiuolo: *Apollo and Daphne*. Another hilarious painting. Apollo fell in lust with Daphne and tried to rape her. Just as he was about to succeed, she was turned into a laurel tree – a story told in the first book of Ovid's *Metamorphoses*. Here her arms – stuck up in the air like enormous lollipops – are already sprouting leaves. She looks suspiciously as if she is smirking at Apollo.

Apollo and Daphne, *Antonio del Pollaiuolo*

Guido Reni: *The Rape of Europa*. The god Zeus had a habit of transforming himself when he wanted to have his way with mortal women. When he decided to impregnate Danaë, for instance, he did it as a shower of gold. In order to have sex with Europa, however, he took the form of a bull. In this painting, she looks as soft-eyed as a cow as, under a lilac sky, Zeus carries her off over the sea to Crete. Eventually she will give birth to three boys – one of whom will grow up to become King Minos.

The Rape of Europa, *Guido Reni, and right,*
The Vestal Virgin Tuccia with a Sieve, *Mantegna*

Mantegna: *The Vestal Virgin Tuccia with a Sieve*. Six vestal virgins attended to the goddess Vesta, protector of the hearth, in Rome. In return for chastity, they had rather a good life – they could own property, they were accorded all kinds of special privileges, and were rather powerful, sometimes being put in charge of important state documents, such as the emperor Augustus's will. Tuccia was accused of being no better than she ought to have been and, to prove her innocence, miraculously carried a quantity of water in a sieve.

The Judgement of Paris, *Rubens,*
probably 1632–35

Rubens: *The Judgement of Paris.* There are two works by Rubens in the same room of the National Gallery, each depicting slightly different moments in this famous story; I prefer the version from the early 1630s where the three goddesses Venus, Minerva and

Juno are parading up and down like beauty queens while Paris takes a good long look at their naked bodies. Juno's peacock struts in the foreground, and Minerva has taken off her armour so that her lovely curves can better be admired. The fury Alecto is hovering overhead, though, to hint at the fact that Paris's choice indirectly causes the Trojan War.

All the poems in this book can be read in translation: some editions usefully come with a Latin and English parallel text.

I recommend *Virgil: The Aeneid*, translated by Robert Fagles (Penguin); *The Poems of Catullus*, translated by James Michie, (parallel text; Random House); *Tibullus: Elegies*, translated by Guy Lee, which also contains the poems of Sulpicia (parallel text, Francis Cairns); WG Shepherd's translation of Propertius (University of Oklahoma Press); and David West's translation of the first book of the Odes of Horace (Oxford University Press).

For Ovid: Peter Green's translations of the *Amores, Ars Amatoria* and *Remedia Amoris* are collected in *Ovid: The Erotic Poems* (Penguin Classics). Christopher Marlowe's lovely translations of Ovid can be found in *Christopher Marlowe: The Complete Poems and Translations. Tales from Ovid: Twenty-four Passages from the Metamorphoses,* translated by Ted Hughes (Farrar, Straus and Giroux), is also well worth looking at. And *The Oxford Book of Classical Verse in Translation* (Oxford University Press), edited by Adrian Poole and Jeremy Maule, includes a great selection of poems and an interesting essay on the perils of translation.

If you want to brush up rusty Latin, Harry Mount's *Amo Amas Amat: How to Become a Latin Lover* (Hyperion), is a hoot.

To get a feel for the period in which the Latin love poets lived, there is no better place to start than *Rubicon* by Tom Holland (Anchor), a gripping account of the collapse of the Roman Republic.

For classical mythology, I like *Children of the Gods* by Kenneth McLeish (Longman), with lovely illustrations by Elisabeth Frink. It's out of print, but you can find second-hand copies on Amazon and Abe. And Robert Graves's *The Greek Myths* (Penguin) is excellent.

I, Claudius, the 1976 BBC drama based on Robert Graves's novels is an absolute classic of television, charting the careers of the Roman emperors from Augustus to the eponymous Claudius. It is based on Suetonius's scurrilous, gossipy *Lives of the Caesars*, which itself is well worth reading in Robert Graves's translation for Penguin Classics. Available as a BBC DVD box set.

Rome, the big-budget HBO/BBC series, brings the period to life brilliantly. Starting as Julius Caesar crosses the Rubicon, its characters' stories are told against the background of the disintegration of the Republic. It has a wonderful cast, sex and violence aplenty, and is incredibly moving. Available on DVD.

ACKNOWLEDGEMENTS

To all at Short Books, especially Rebecca Nicolson and Vanessa Webb, who nurtured this project from the start; and to Rakesh Satyal and Rob Crawford at HarperCollins, who took it on in the U.S.

To Peter Straus; and to George Lucas.

To my colleagues at the *Guardian*; especially Nick Hopkins and Alan Rusbridger.

To Cynthia Smart, Jasper Griffin, the late Michael Comber and most particularly the late Oliver Lyne, who all taught me to love Latin poetry.

To my family, especially Peter and Pamela Higgins.

To my friends Richard Baker, Andy Beckett, James Davidson, Paul Laity, Frank Lampen, Ginny Macbeth, Jacqueline Riding and Rosie Toop. Most especially to Joshua St Johnston for countless brilliant suggestions and for cheering me on.

To Matthew Fox: "*carmina quis potuit tuto legisse Tibulli/vel tua, cuius opus Cynthia sola fuit?/quis poterit lecto durus discedere Gallo?/et mea nescio quid carmina tale sonant.*"

The mistakes are all my own.

Index